ARE WE FEELING SAFER YET?

A (th)ink ANTHOLOGY

ARE WE SAFER

CARTOONS BY KEITH KNIGHT

KEITH KNIGHT PRESS

FEELING YET?

A (th)ink ANTHOLOGY

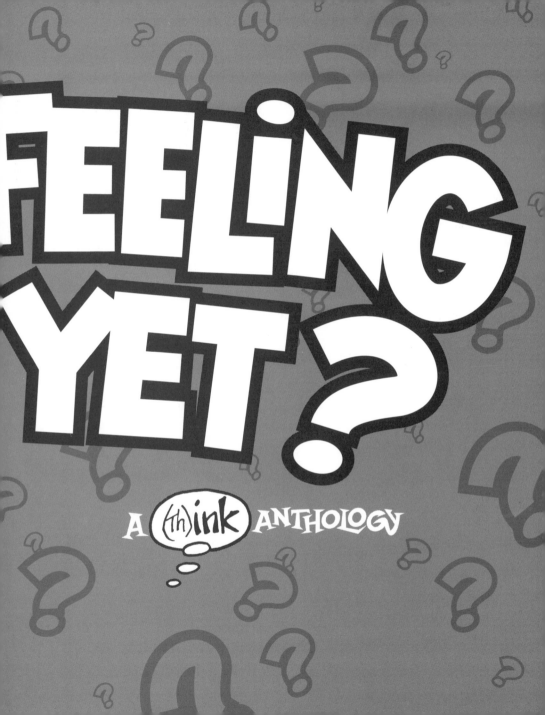

Dedicated to the men and women who have lost their lives unnecessarily during this ugly moment in American history. We will never forget your sacrifice.

Thanks to all the editors & readers that support the strip; to Jason for his damn fine skills; to Chris Staros, Dave Eggers & everyone else who helped me out with this self-publishing thing; to Mr. Mansbach, Dr. King , Mr. X and Mr. Chang for their great quotes; to my family; and, most of all, thanks to my lovely wife Kerstin...*kiss*

Also by Keith Knight: *Dances with Sheep; Fear of a Black Marker;*
What a Long Strange Strip It's Been;
Red, White, Black & Blue, The Passion of the Keef;
The Beginner's Guide to Community-Based Arts

ISBN-13: 978-0-9788053-0-2
ISBN-10:   0-9788053-0-5

It is your patriotic duty to send correspondence to Keith Knight P.O. Box 591794, San Francisco CA 94159-1794. keef@kchronicles.com. www.kchronicles.com Design by Jason Chandler at Favorite Studios, Inc.

Printed in Canada

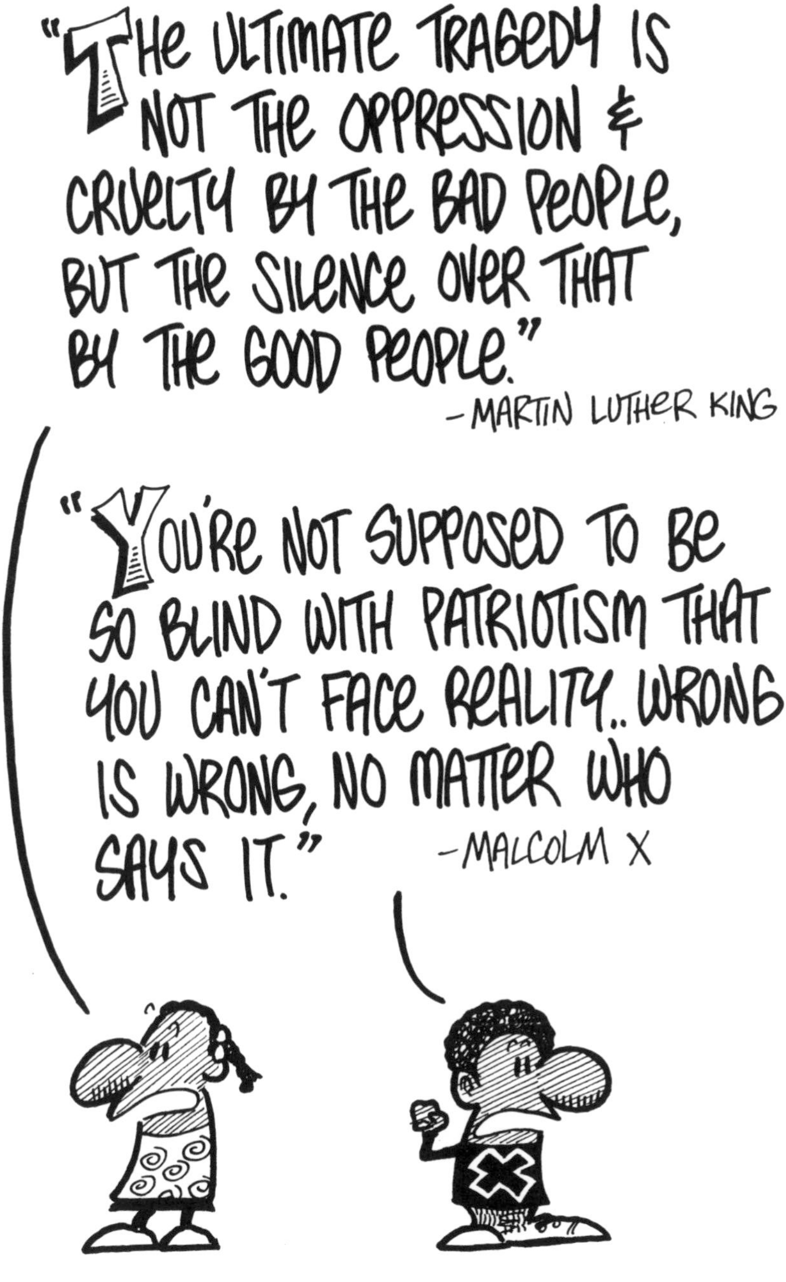
"THE ULTIMATE TRAGEDY IS NOT THE OPPRESSION & CRUELTY BY THE BAD PEOPLE, BUT THE SILENCE OVER THAT BY THE GOOD PEOPLE."
-MARTIN LUTHER KING
"YOU'RE NOT SUPPOSED TO BE SO BLIND WITH PATRIOTISM THAT YOU CAN'T FACE REALITY.. WRONG IS WRONG, NO MATTER WHO SAYS IT."
-MALCOLM X

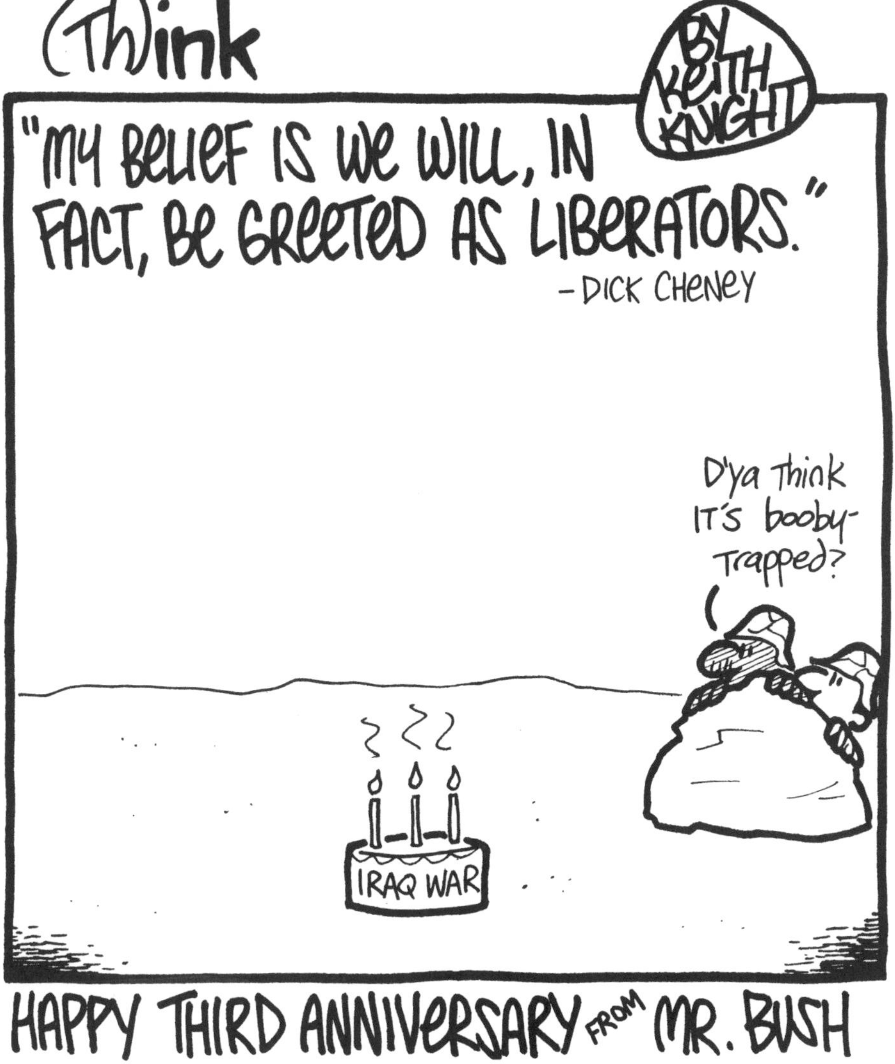
(Th)ink
BY KEITH KNIGHT
"MY BELIEF IS WE WILL, IN FACT, BE GREETED AS LIBERATORS."
-DICK CHENEY
D'ya Think IT'S booby-Trapped?
IRAQ WAR
HAPPY THIRD ANNIVERSARY FROM MR. BUSH

(th)ink

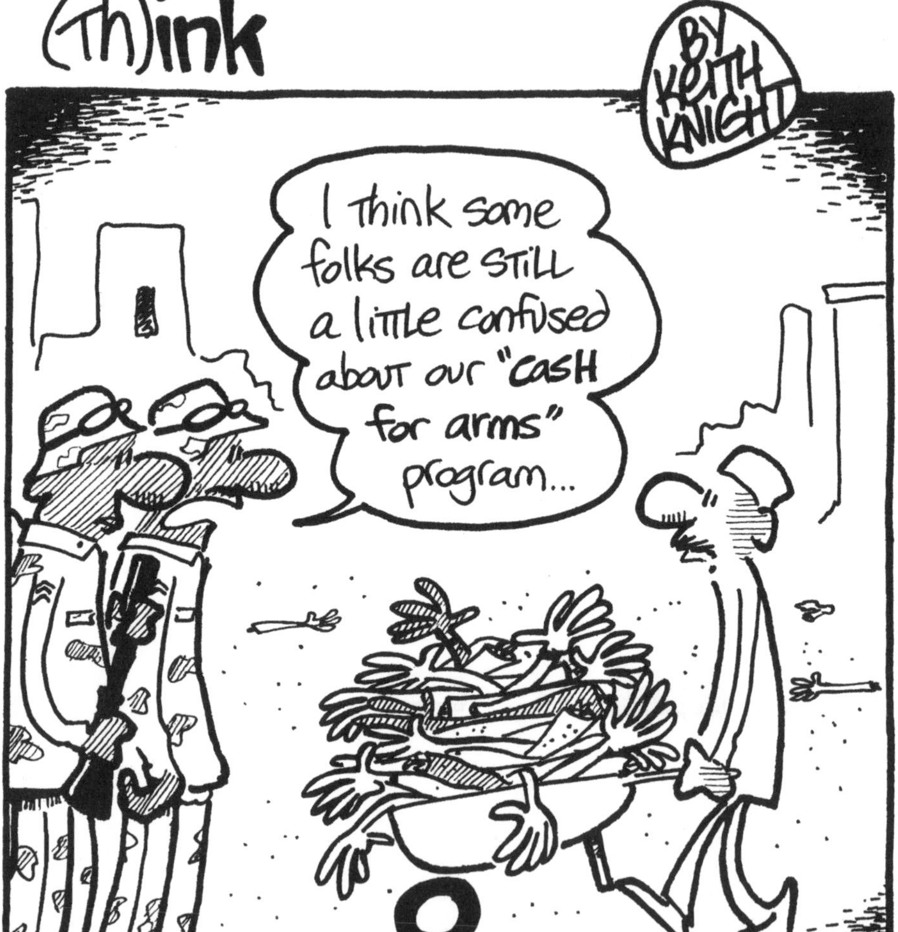
BY KEITH KNIGHT
I think some folks are STILL a little confused about our "CASH for arms" program...

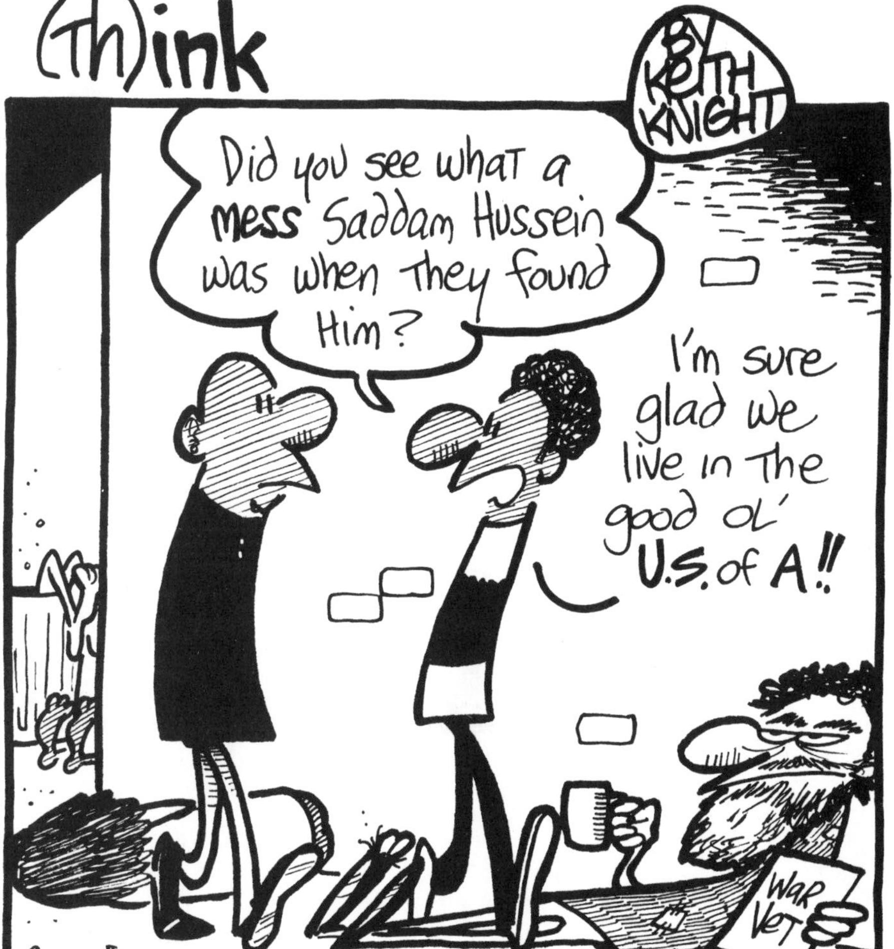
(th)ink
BY KEITH KNIGHT
Did you see what a mess Saddam Hussein was when they found him?
I'm sure glad we live in the good ol' U.S. of A!!
WAR VET

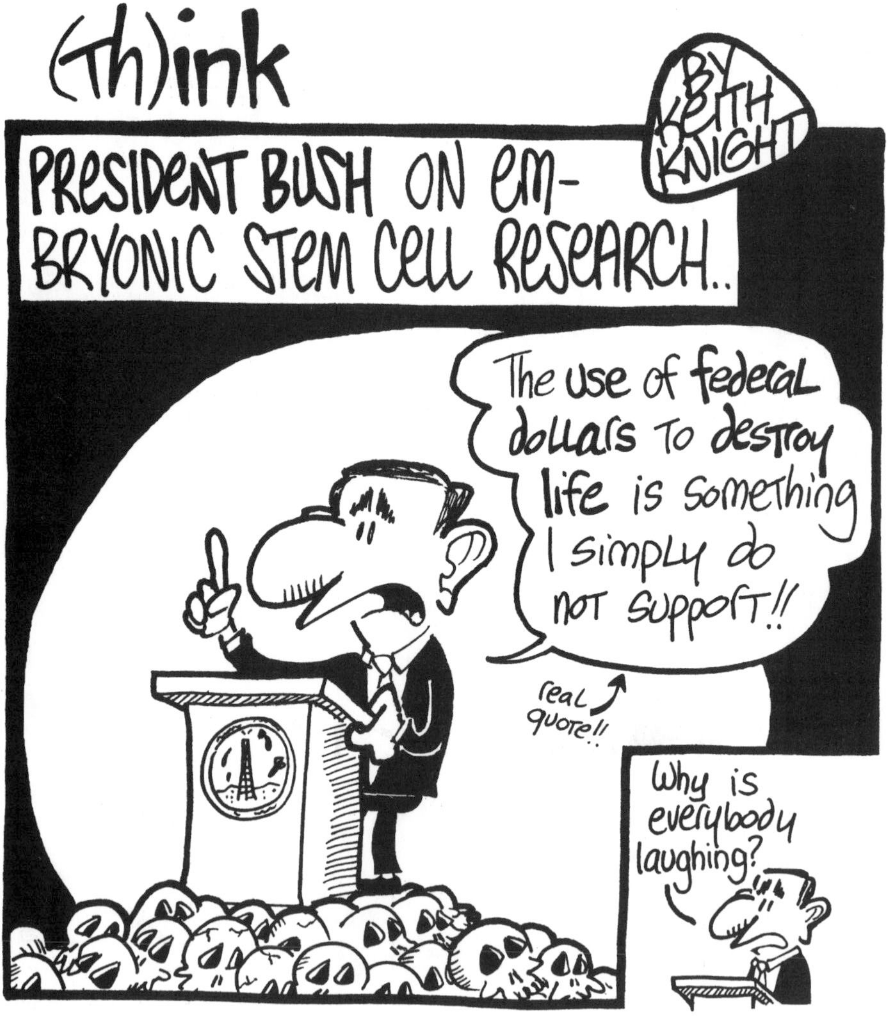
(Th)ink
BY KEITH KNIGHT
PRESIDENT BUSH ON EMBRYONIC STEM CELL RESEARCH..
The use of federal dollars to destroy life is something I simply do not support!!
real quote!!
Why is everybody laughing?

(Th)ink
BY KEITH KNIGHT
NEWS ITEM: ARMY COMMAND SGT. MAJOR JAMES JORDAN, BROTHER OF MICHAEL JORDAN, HAS ASKED TO STAY IN THE ARMY FOR A YEAR BEYOND HIS MANDATORY RETIREMENT DATE, TO SERVE IN IRAQ...
U.S.A.
Not knowing when it's time to quit must run in the family!!

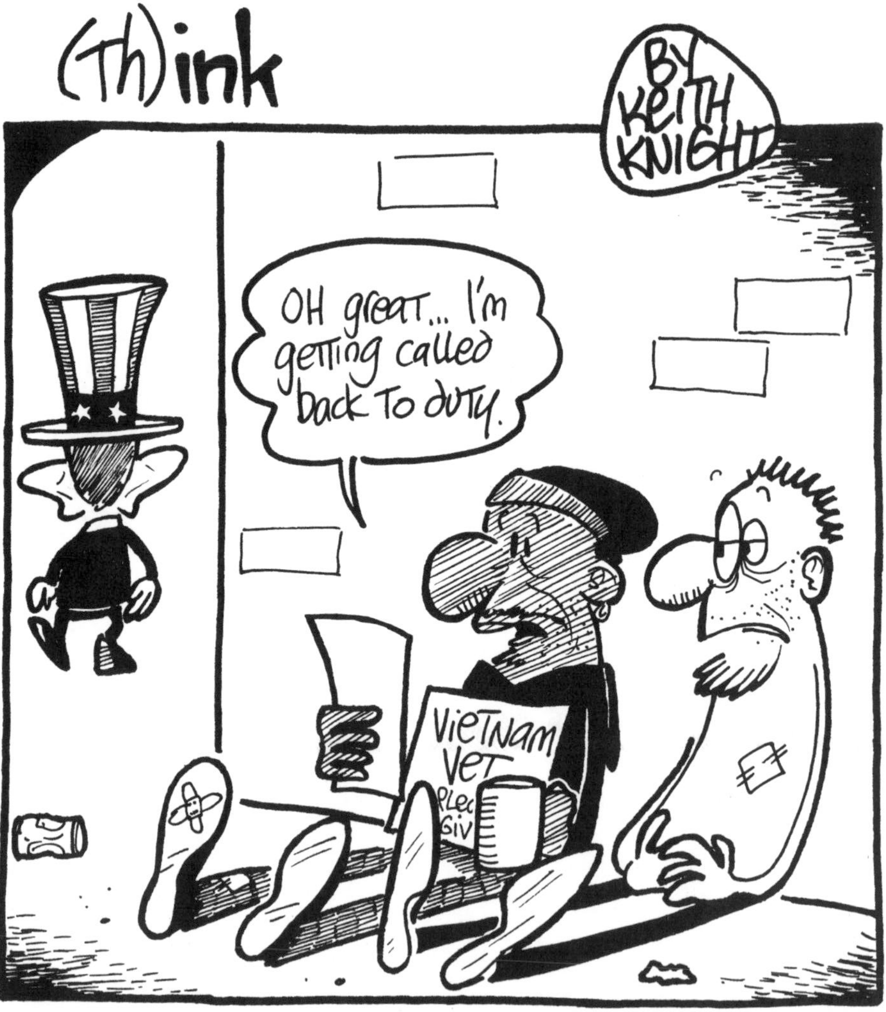
(TH)INK
BY KEITH KNIGHT
OH GREAT... I'M GETTING CALLED BACK TO DUTY.
VIETNAM VET
BUSH QUIETLY TACKLES HOMELESS PROBLEM

(Th)ink
BY KEITH KNIGHT
NEWS ITEM: WITH RECRUITMENT LEVELS AT NEAR-RECORD LOWS, THE U.S. MILITARY MAKES A DESPERATE ATTEMPT TO APPEAL TO THE HIP-HOP GENERATION...
RECRUITMENT OFFICE
We've hired Karrine Steffans as our Head recruiter..

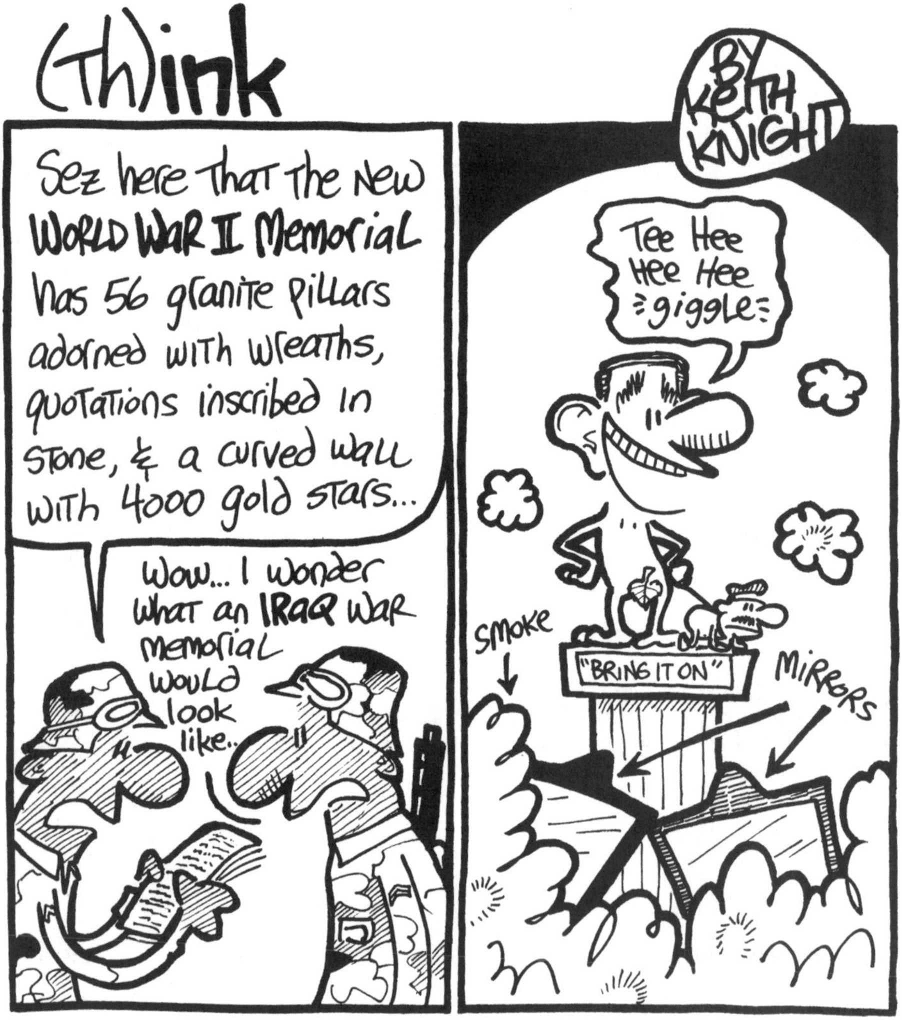
(Th)ink
By Keith Knight
Sez here that the new WORLD WAR II Memorial has 56 granite pillars adorned with wreaths, quotations inscribed in stone, & a curved wall with 4000 gold stars...
Wow... I wonder what an IRAQ War memorial would look like..
Tee Hee Hee Hee giggle
"BRING IT ON"
SMOKE
MIRRORS

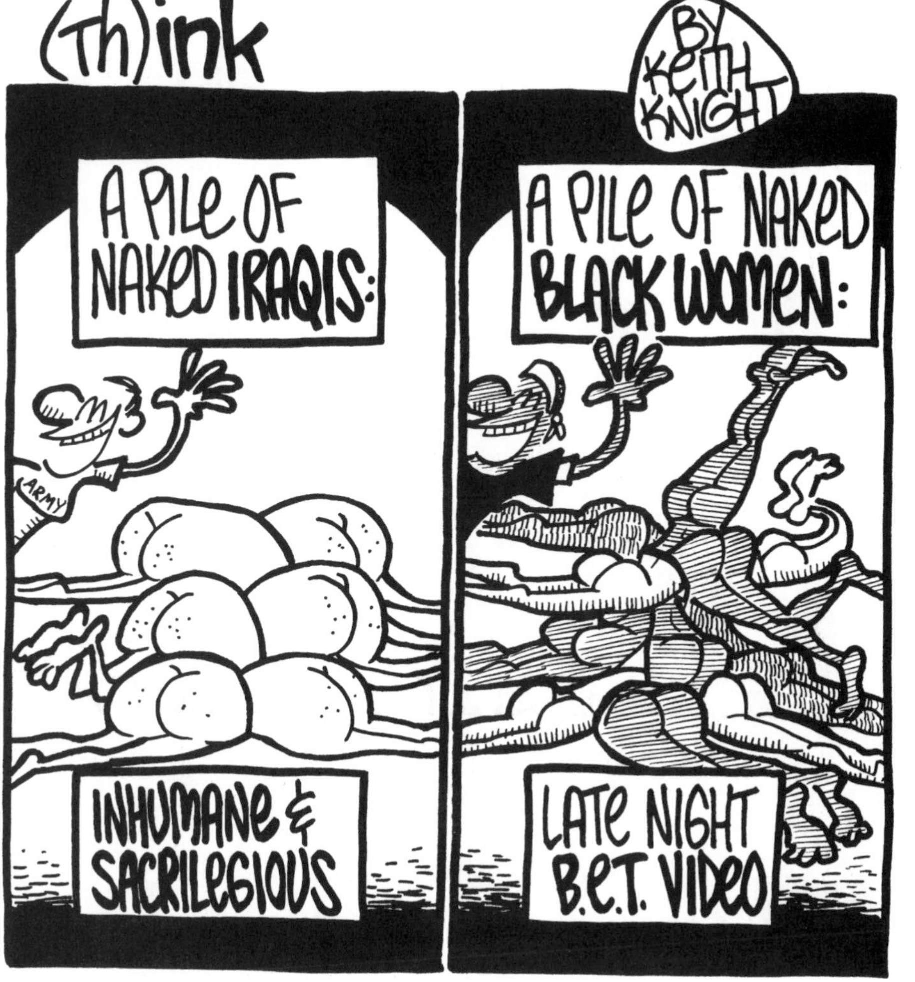
(TH)INK
BY KEITH KNIGHT
A PILE OF NAKED IRAQIS:
ARMY
INHUMANE & SACRILEGIOUS
A PILE OF NAKED BLACK WOMEN:
LATE NIGHT B.E.T. VIDEO

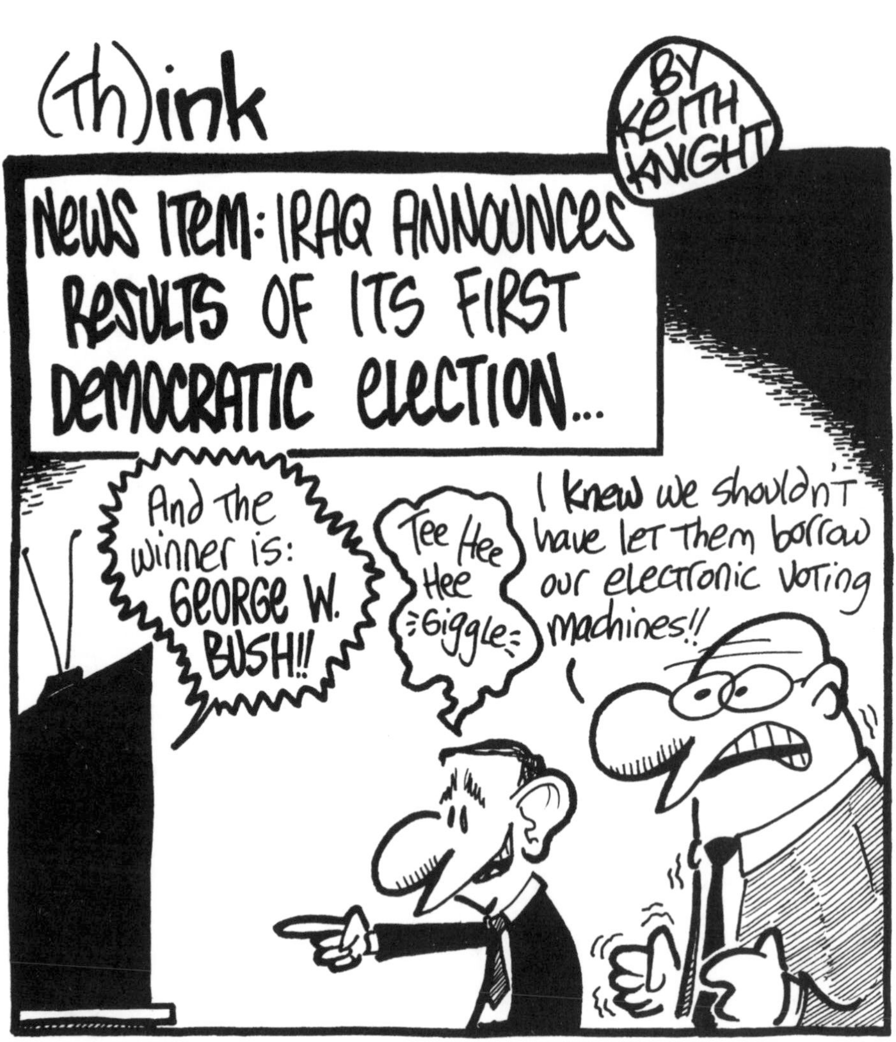
(Th)ink
BY KEITH KNIGHT
NEWS ITEM: IRAQ ANNOUNCES RESULTS OF ITS FIRST DEMOCRATIC ELECTION...
And the winner is: GEORGE W. BUSH!!
Tee Hee Hee Giggle
I knew we shouldn't have let them borrow our electronic voting machines!!

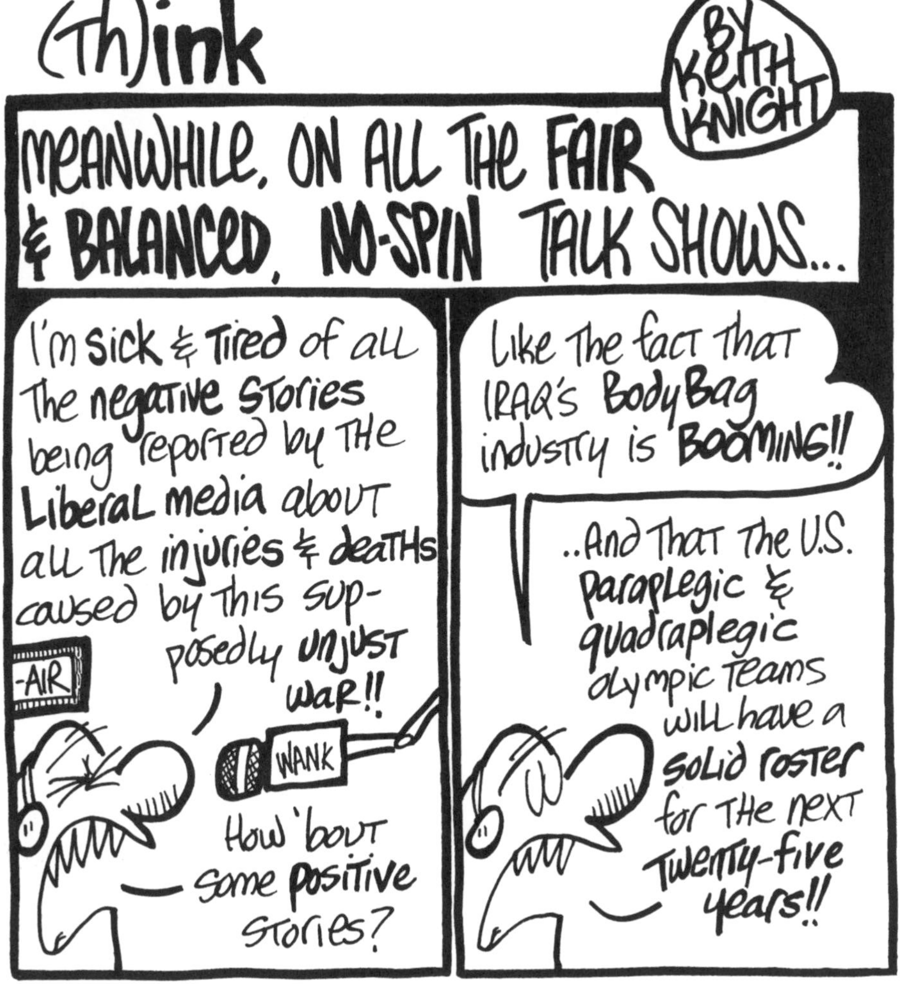
(Th)ink
BY KEITH KNIGHT
MEANWHILE, ON ALL THE FAIR & BALANCED, NO-SPIN TALK SHOWS...
I'm sick & tired of all the negative stories being reported by the Liberal media about all the injuries & deaths caused by this sup-posedly unjust war!!
-AIR
WANK
How 'bout some positive stories?
Like the fact that Iraq's Body Bag industry is BOOMING!!
..And that the U.S. paraplegic & quadraplegic olympic teams will have a solid roster for the next twenty-five years!!

(Th)ink

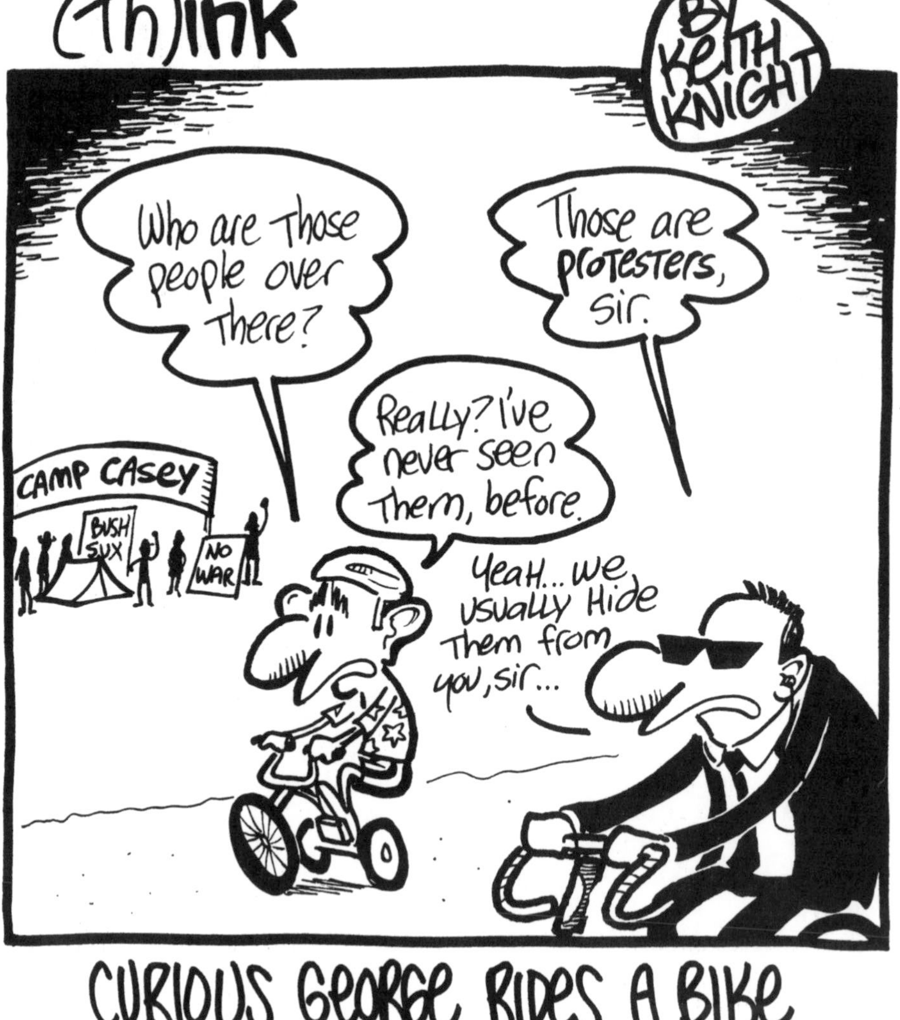
By Keith Knight
Who are those people over there?
Those are protesters, sir.
Really? I've never seen them, before.
Yeah... we usually hide them from you, sir...
CAMP CASEY
BUSH SUX
NO WAR

CURIOUS GEORGE RIDES A BIKE

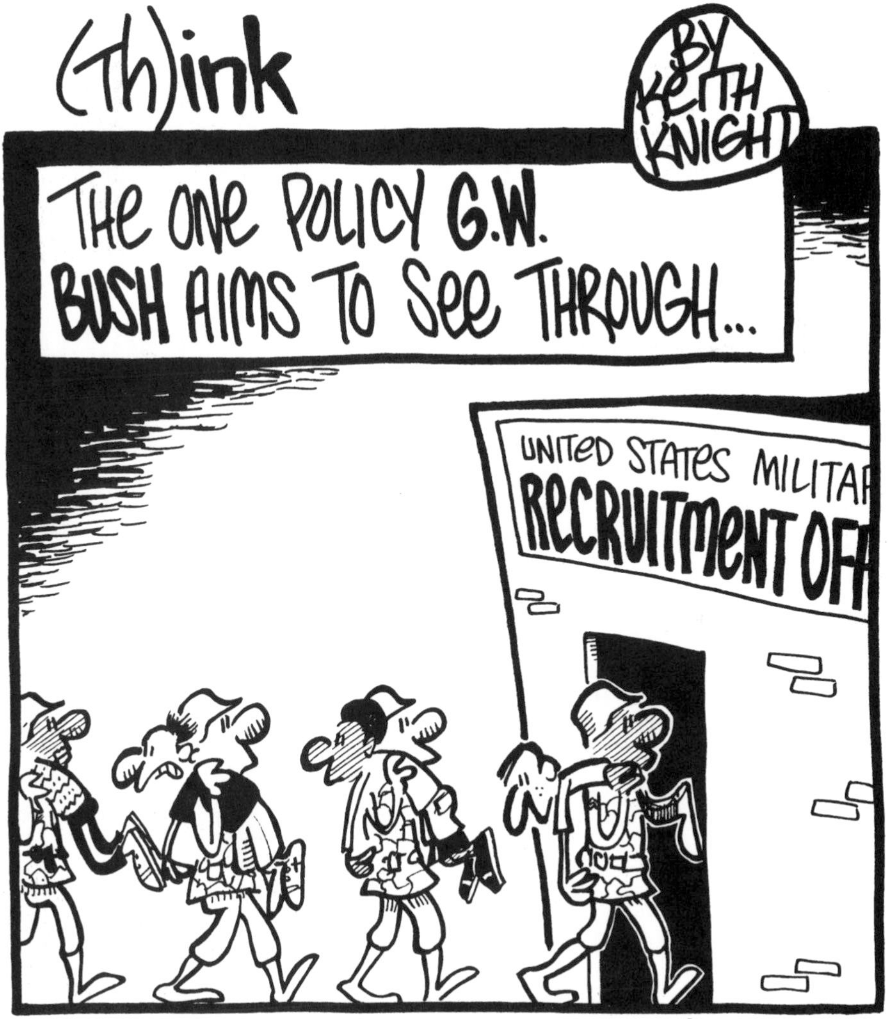
(Th)ink
BY KEITH KNIGHT
THE ONE POLICY G.W. BUSH AIMS TO SEE THROUGH...
UNITED STATES MILITAR
RECRUITMENT OFF
NO CHILD LEFT BEHIND

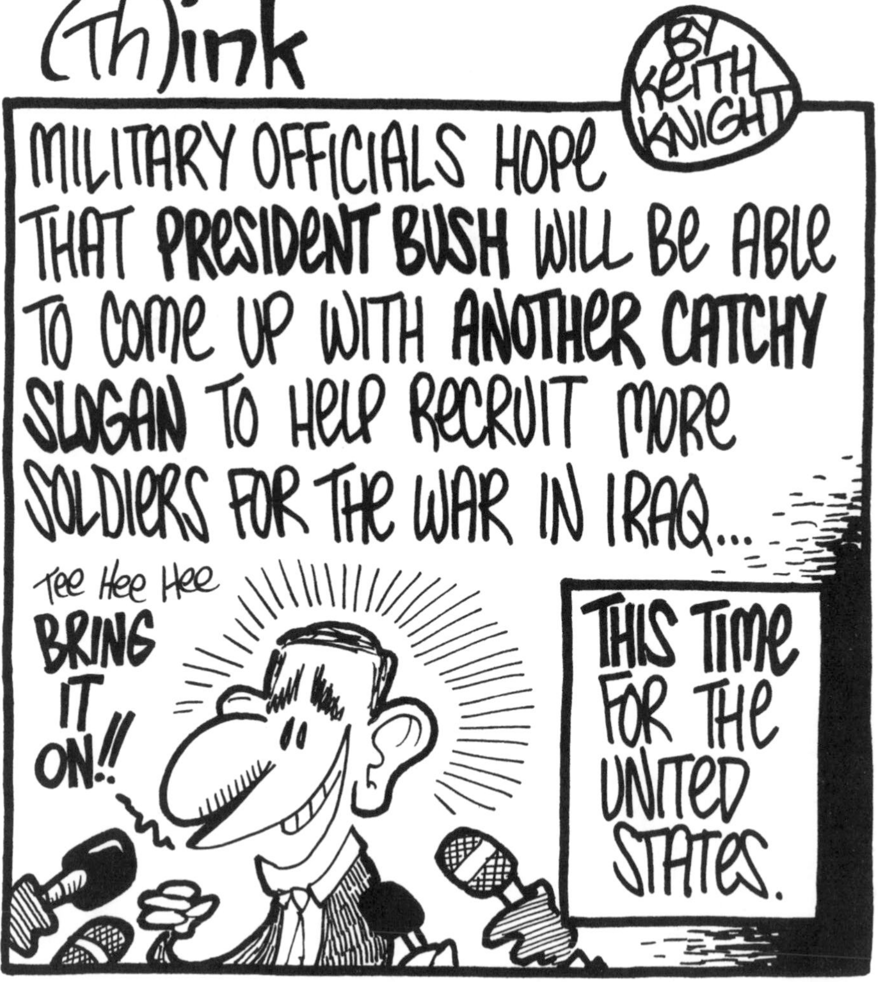
(Th)ink
BY KEITH KNIGHT
MILITARY OFFICIALS HOPE THAT PRESIDENT BUSH WILL BE ABLE TO COME UP WITH ANOTHER CATCHY SLOGAN TO HELP RECRUIT MORE SOLDIERS FOR THE WAR IN IRAQ...
Tee Hee Hee
BRING IT ON!!
THIS TIME FOR THE UNITED STATES.

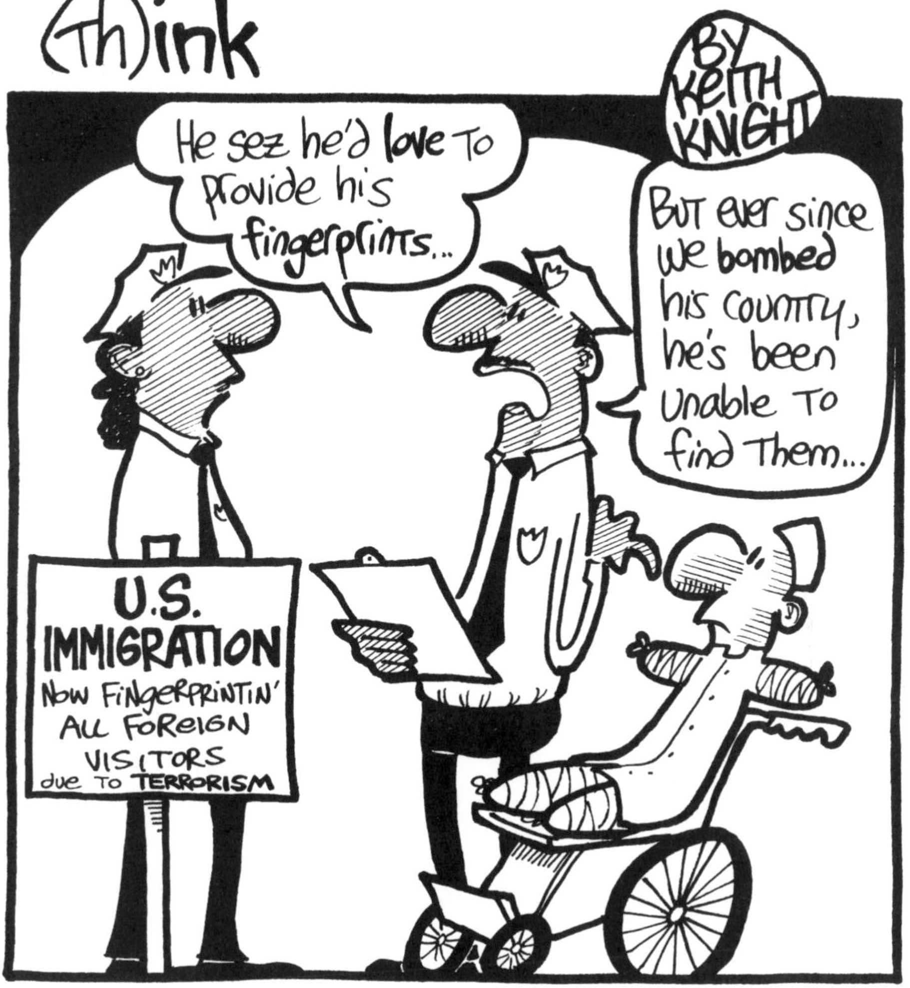
(Th)ink
By Keith Knight
He sez he'd **love** to provide his **fingerprints**...
But ever since we **bombed** his country, he's been unable to find them...
U.S. IMMIGRATION
Now Fingerprintin' All Foreign Visitors due to TERRORISM

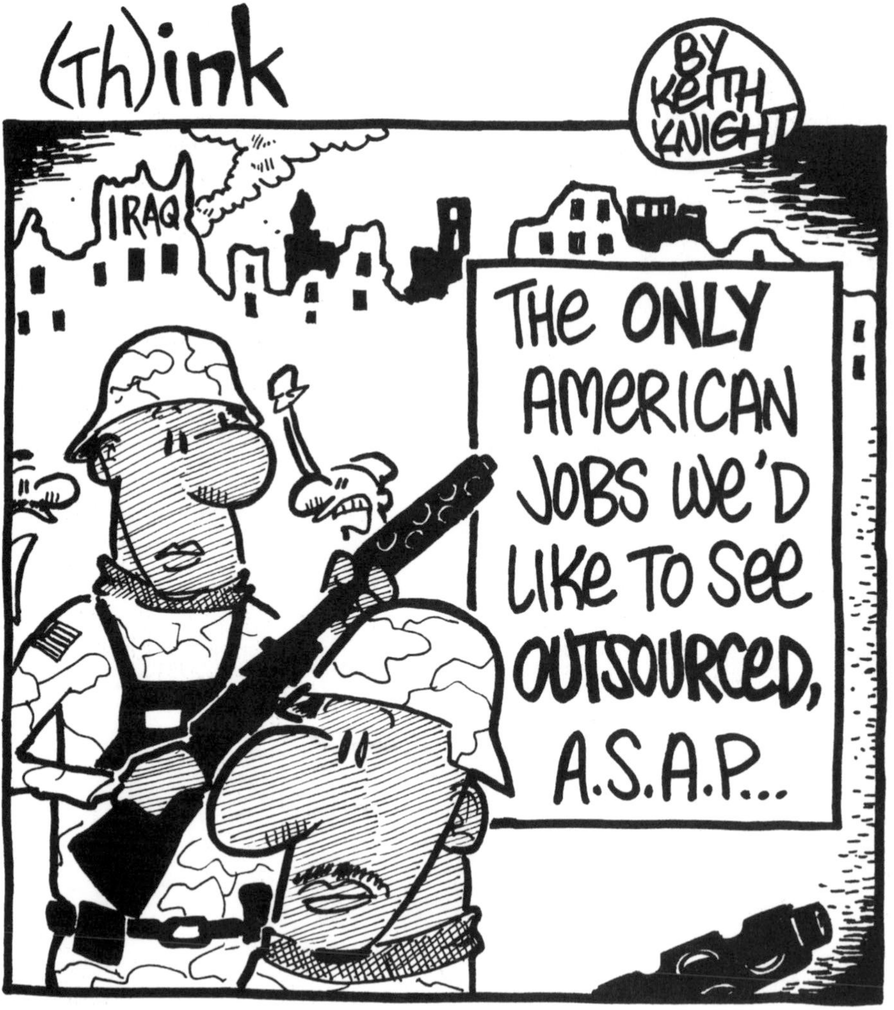
(Th)ink
BY KEITH KNIGHT
IRAQ
THE ONLY AMERICAN JOBS WE'D LIKE TO SEE OUTSOURCED, A.S.A.P...

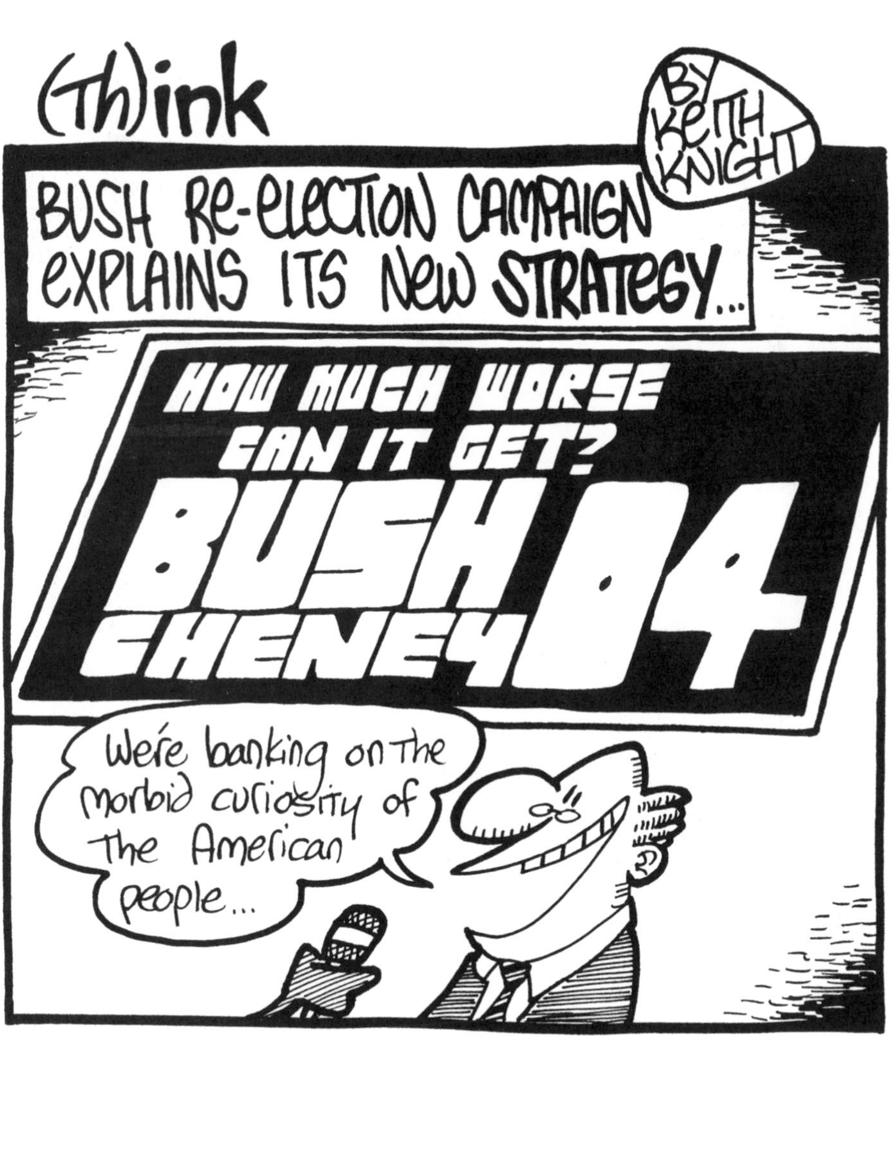
(Th)ink
BY KEITH KNIGHT
BUSH Re-ELECTION CAMPAIGN EXPLAINS ITS New STRATEGY...
HOW MUCH WORSE CAN IT GET?
BUSH CHENEY 04
We're banking on the morbid curiosity of the American people...

(Th)ink
BY KEITH KNIGHT
NEWS ITEM: FLORIDA GOVERNOR JEB BUSH TOUTS ADVANCED TECHNOLOGY BROUGHT IN TO HANDLE THE INCREASED AFRICAN-AMERICAN VOTE SINCE THE LAST ELECTION...
2000
ULTRA-SHREDDER 28000
NOW

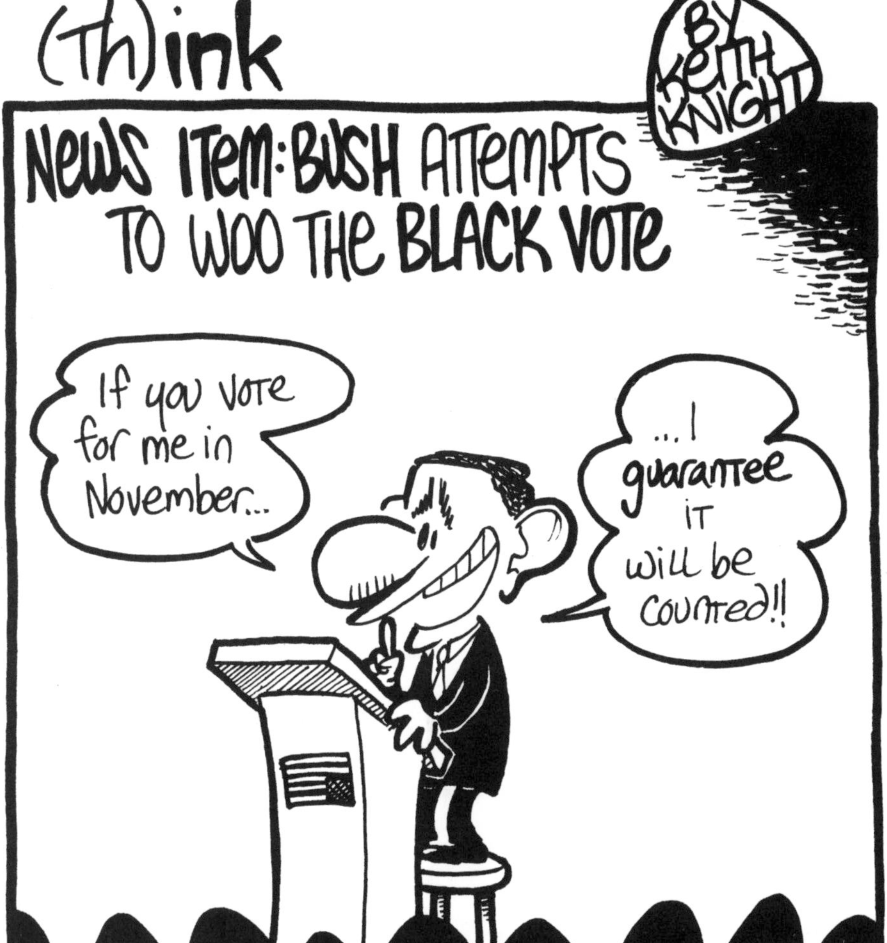
(Th)ink
BY KEITH KNIGHT
NEWS ITEM: BUSH ATTEMPTS TO WOO THE BLACK VOTE
If you vote for me in November...
...I guarantee it will be counted!!

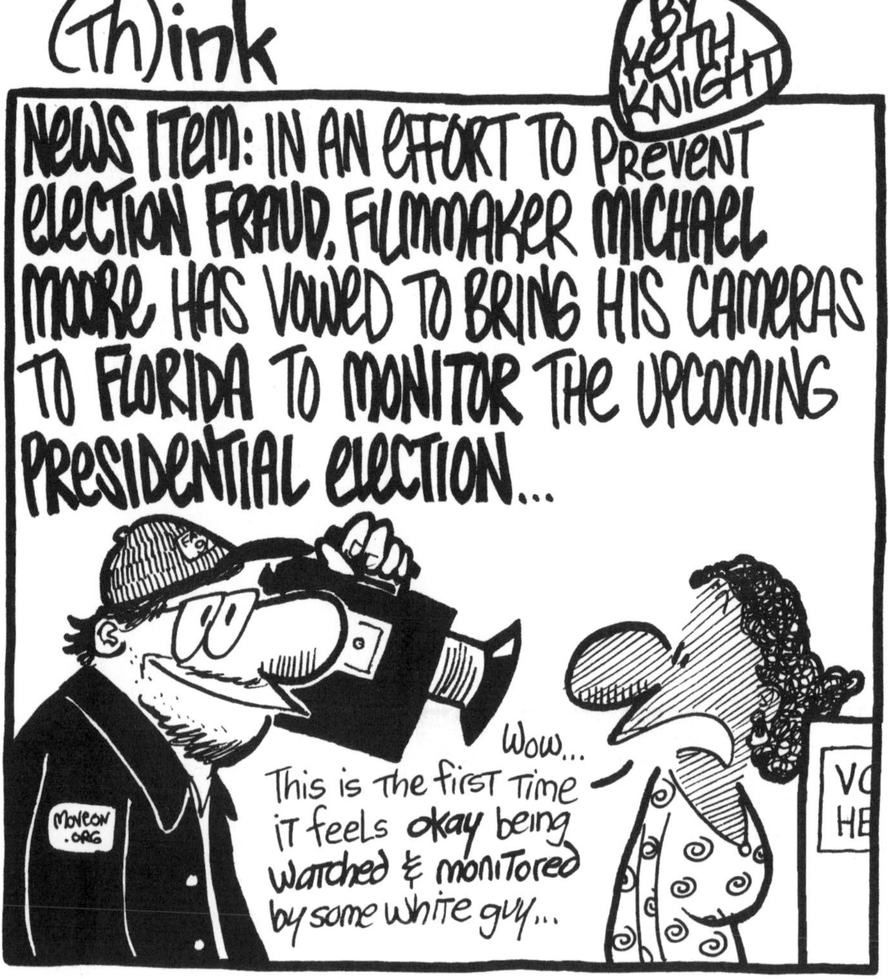

(th)ink
BY KEITH KNIGHT
NEWS ITEM: IN AN EFFORT TO PREVENT ELECTION FRAUD, FILMMAKER MICHAEL MOORE HAS VOWED TO BRING HIS CAMERAS TO FLORIDA TO MONITOR THE UPCOMING PRESIDENTIAL ELECTION...
MOVEON .ORG
Wow... This is the first time it feels okay being watched & monitored by some white guy...

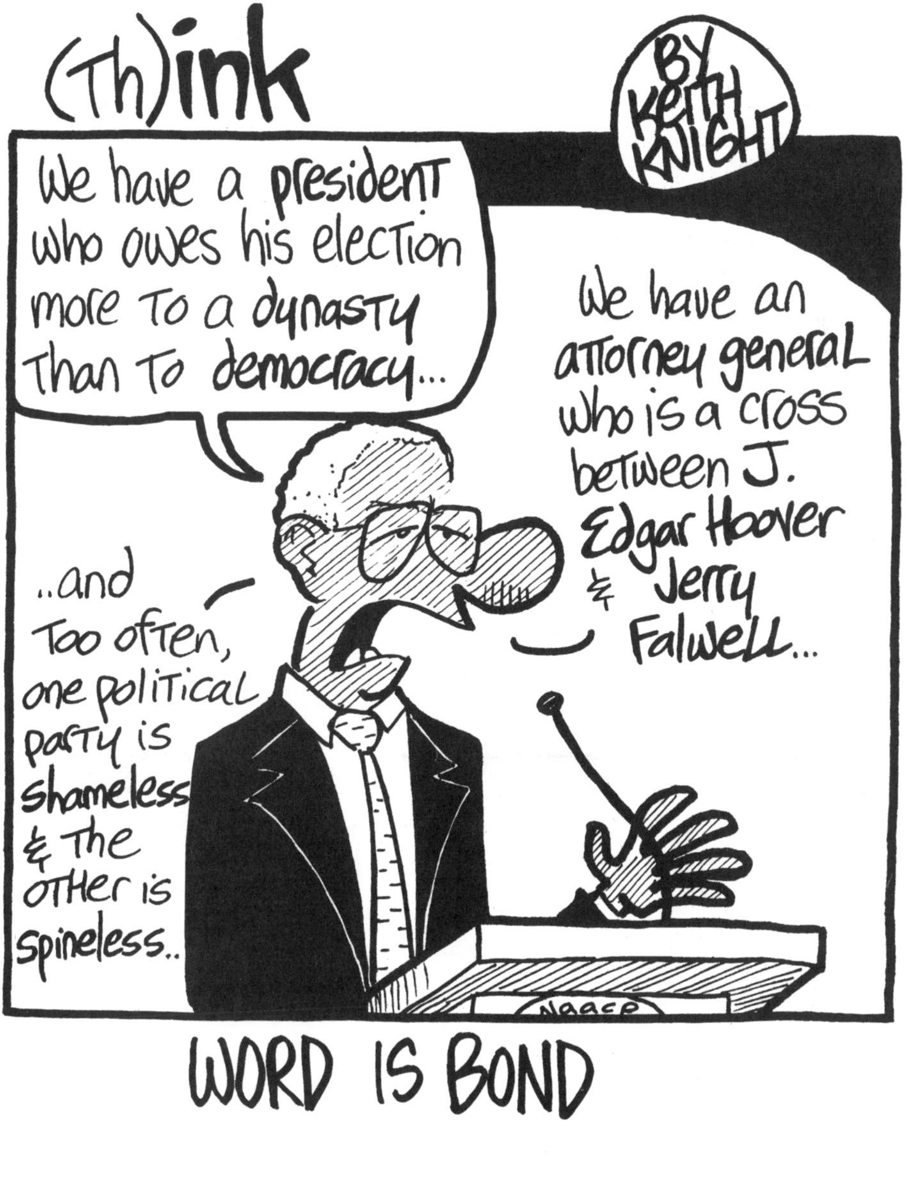
(Th)ink
BY KEITH KNIGHT
We have a president who owes his election more to a dynasty than to democracy...
We have an attorney general who is a cross between J. Edgar Hoover & Jerry Falwell...
..and too often, one political party is shameless & the other is spineless..
WORD IS BOND

(Th)ink
By Keith Knight
News Item: Bush still attempting to explain mysterious bulge seen during debates....
Any truth to the rumor that Dick is telling you what to do?

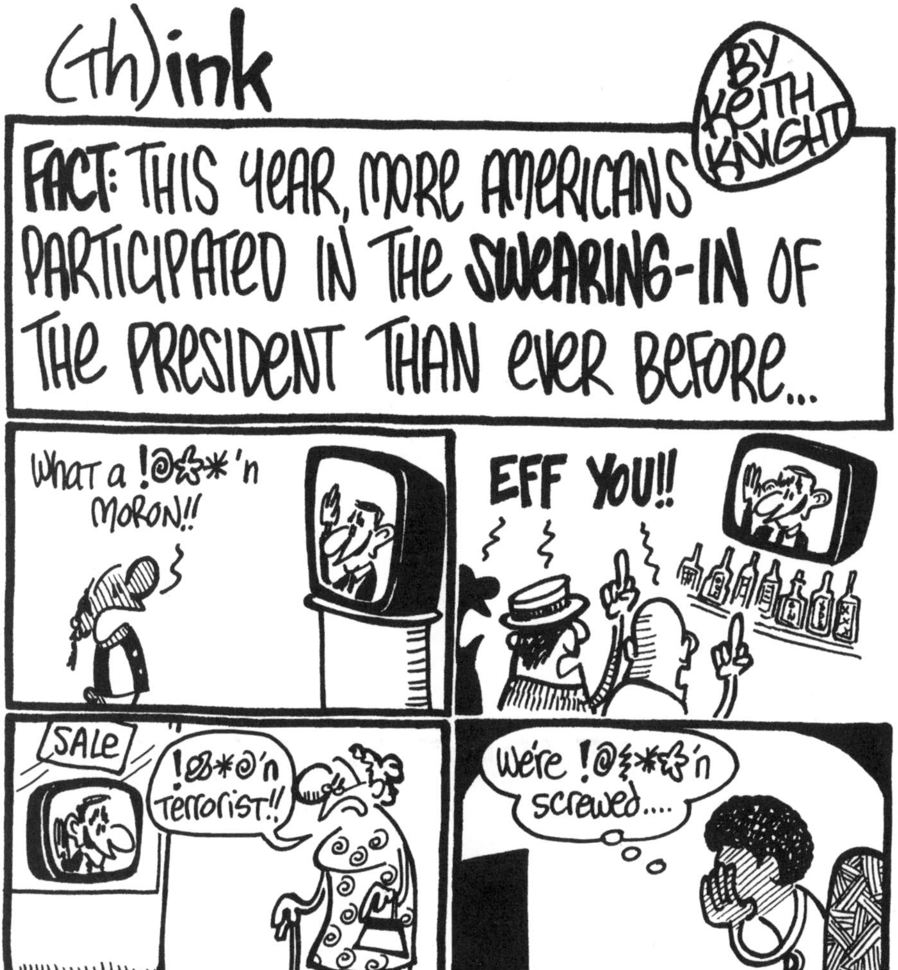
(th)ink
BY KEITH KNIGHT
FACT: THIS YEAR, MORE AMERICANS PARTICIPATED IN THE SWEARING-IN OF THE PRESIDENT THAN EVER BEFORE...
What a !@✿*'n MORON!!
EFF YOU!!
SALE
!✿*@'n Terrorist!!
We're !@*✿'n screwed....

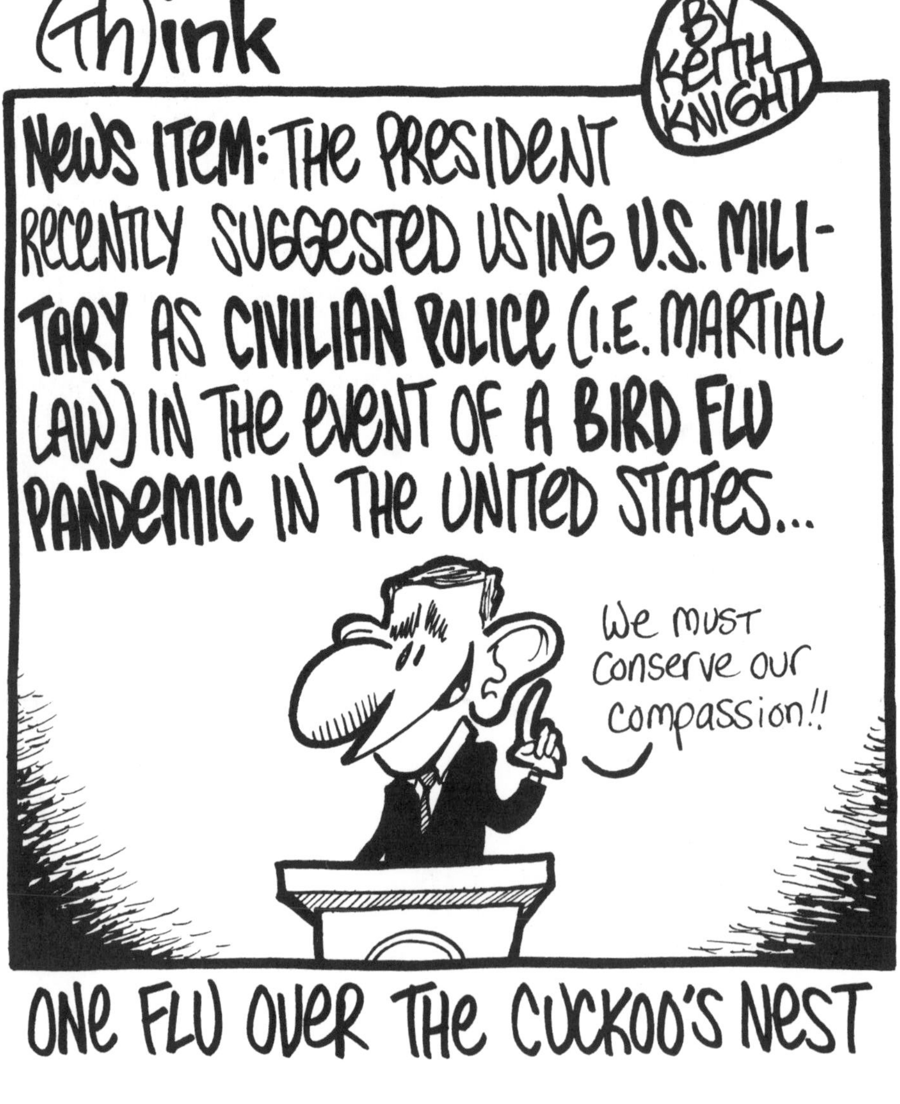
(Th)ink
BY KEITH KNIGHT
NEWS ITEM: THE PRESIDENT RECENTLY SUGGESTED USING U.S. MILITARY AS CIVILIAN POLICE (I.E. MARTIAL LAW) IN THE EVENT OF A BIRD FLU PANDEMIC IN THE UNITED STATES...
We must conserve our compassion!!
ONE FLU OVER THE CUCKOO'S NEST

(Th)ink
BY KEITH KNIGHT
NEWS ITEM: THE AMERICAN BALD EAGLE MAY SOON COME OFF THE ENDANGERED SPECIES LIST..
...& pretty soon, The metaphor will be complete.

(TH)ink
BY KEITH KNIGHT
MOST LIKELY REASON FOR FLORIDA'S DEVASTATING HURRICANE SEASON
Hey, Mother Nature...
BRING IT ON!!

(Th)ink

BY KEITH KNIGHT
NEWS ITEM: PRESIDENT BUSH RESPONDS TO ALL THE FOLKS WHO'VE SQUEALED ABOUT HIS ADMINISTRATION'S POLICIES
TORTURE, ILLEGAL
WIRET
LEAKS, FAILURE TO REACT
TRINA, FAULTY INTELLIGE
NO EXIT STRATEGY, FAKE
VALISTS, ELECTION FRAUD,
, CRONYISM, ETC.
STOP SNITCHIN'

(th)ink
BY KEITH KNIGHT
Hmmm... Mebbe I should do something about this Global warming thing...

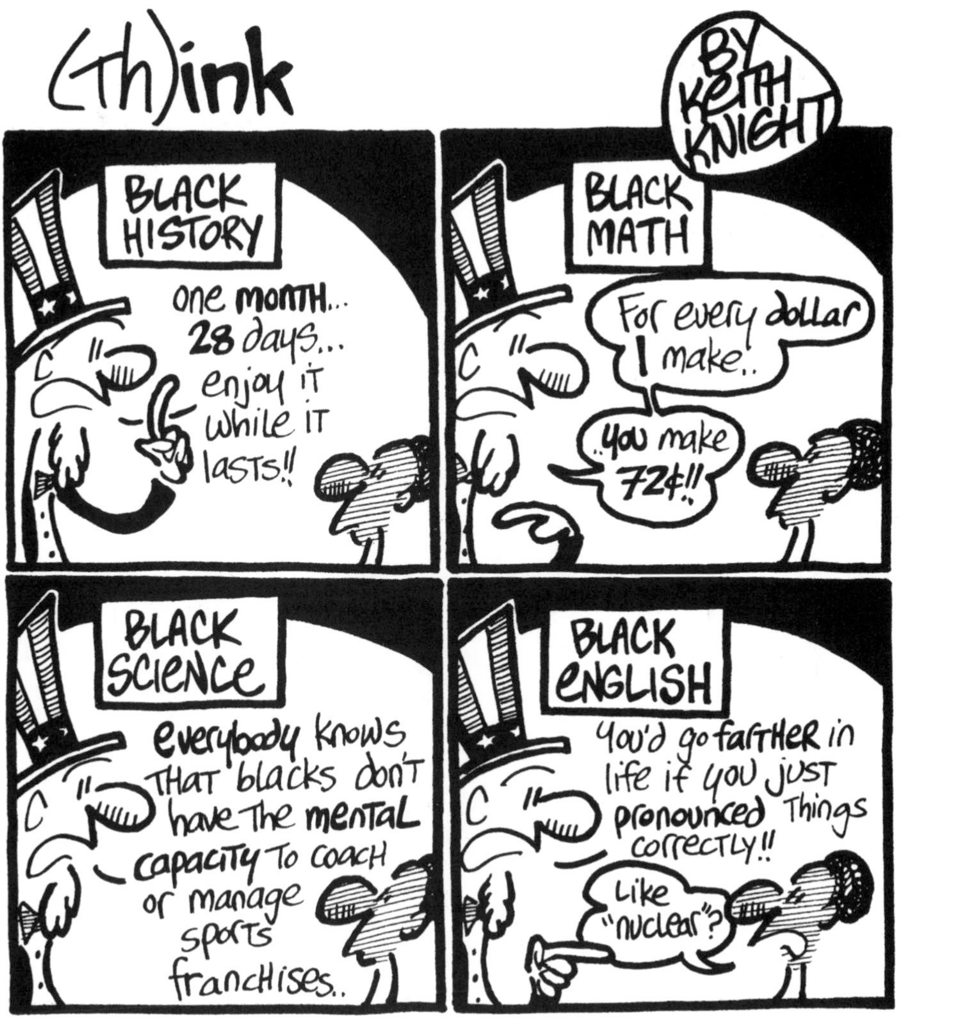

(th)ink
BY KEITH KNIGHT
BLACK HISTORY
one month... 28 days... enjoy it while it lasts!!
BLACK MATH
For every dollar I make..
..you make 72¢!!
BLACK SCIENCE
everybody knows that blacks don't have the mental capacity to coach or manage sports franchises..
BLACK ENGLISH
You'd go farther in life if you just pronounced things correctly!!
Like "nuclear"?

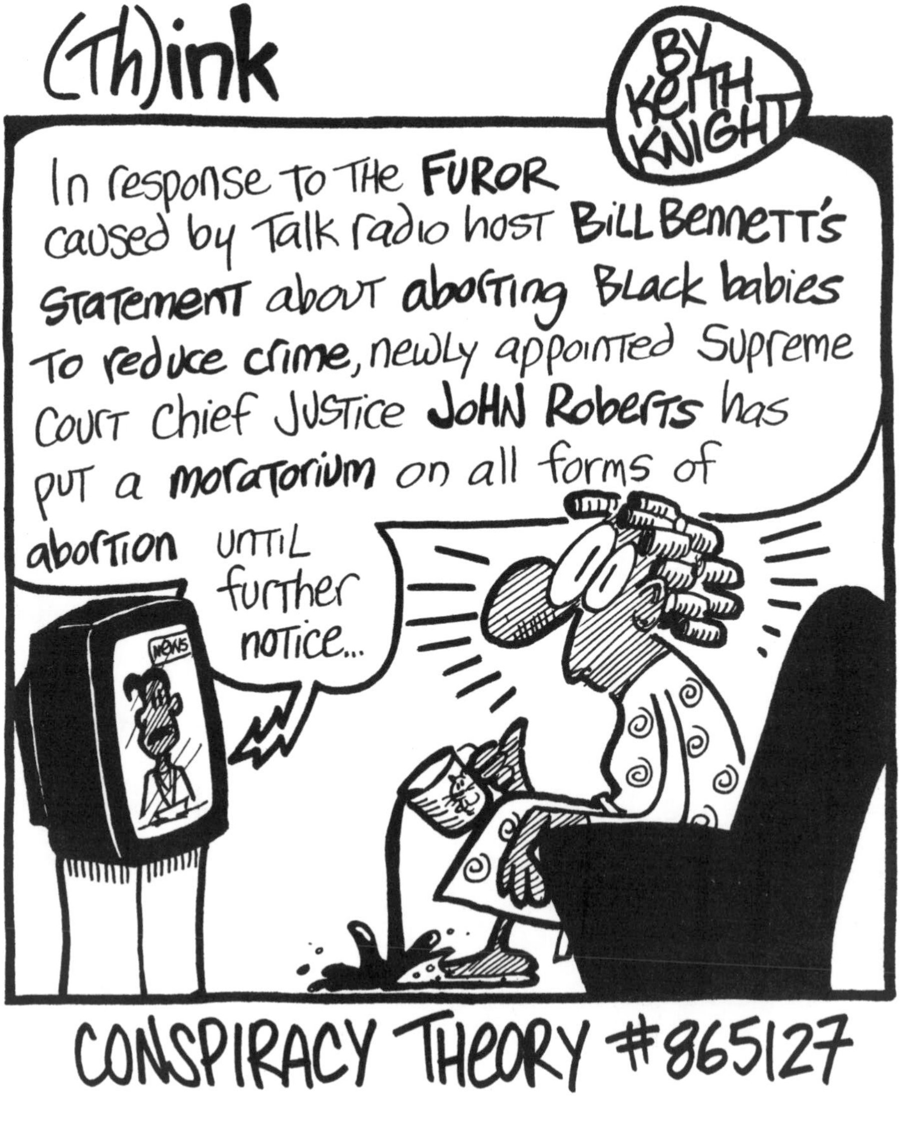
(Th)ink
BY KEITH KNIGHT
In response to the FUROR caused by Talk radio host BILL BENNETT's STATEMENT about aborting Black babies to reduce crime, newly appointed Supreme Court Chief Justice JOHN Roberts has put a moratorium on all forms of abortion until further notice...
NEWS
CONSPIRACY THEORY #865127

(Th)ink
BY KEITH KNIGHT
NEWS ITEM: FLORIDA SENATOR AL LAWSON IS SEEKING A 2¢ PER ROLL TAX ON TOILET PAPER..

PAY AS YOU GO

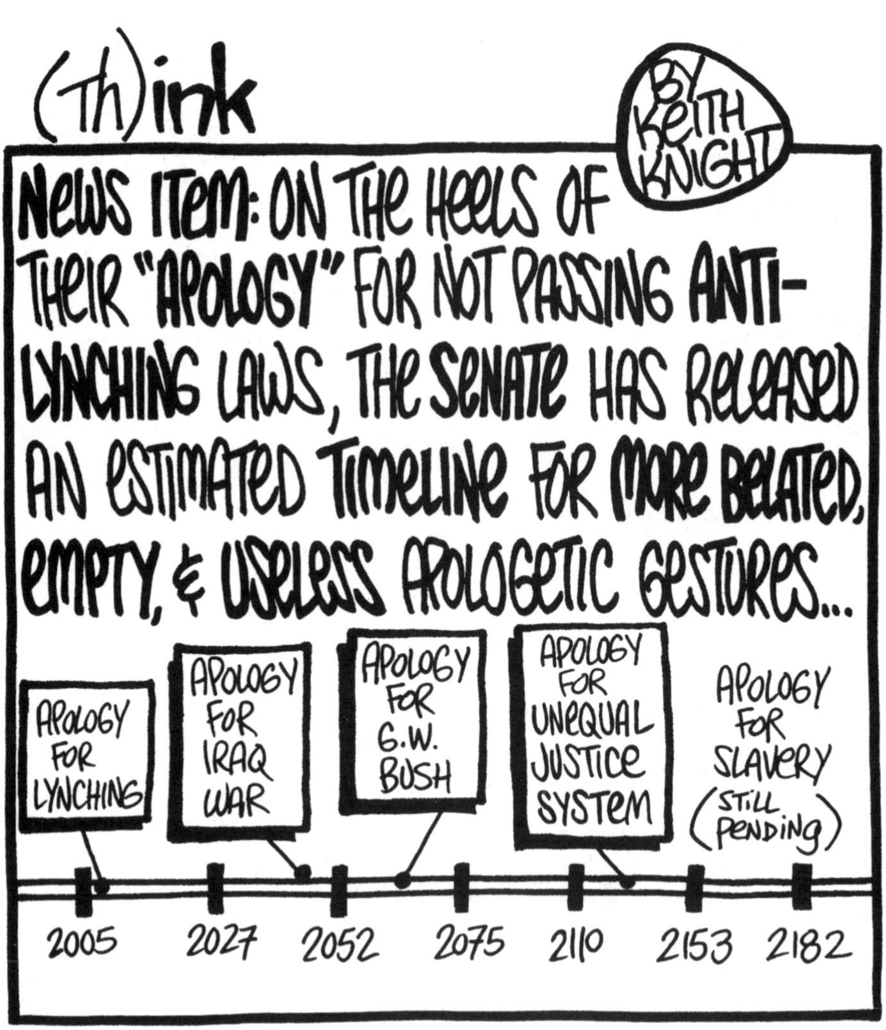
(th)ink
BY KEITH KNIGHT
NEWS ITEM: ON THE HEELS OF THEIR "APOLOGY" FOR NOT PASSING ANTI-LYNCHING LAWS, THE SENATE HAS RELEASED AN ESTIMATED TIMELINE FOR MORE BELATED, EMPTY, & USELESS APOLOGETIC GESTURES...
APOLOGY FOR LYNCHING
APOLOGY FOR IRAQ WAR
APOLOGY FOR G.W. BUSH
APOLOGY FOR UNEQUAL JUSTICE SYSTEM
APOLOGY FOR SLAVERY (STILL PENDING)
2005
2027
2052
2075
2110
2153
2182

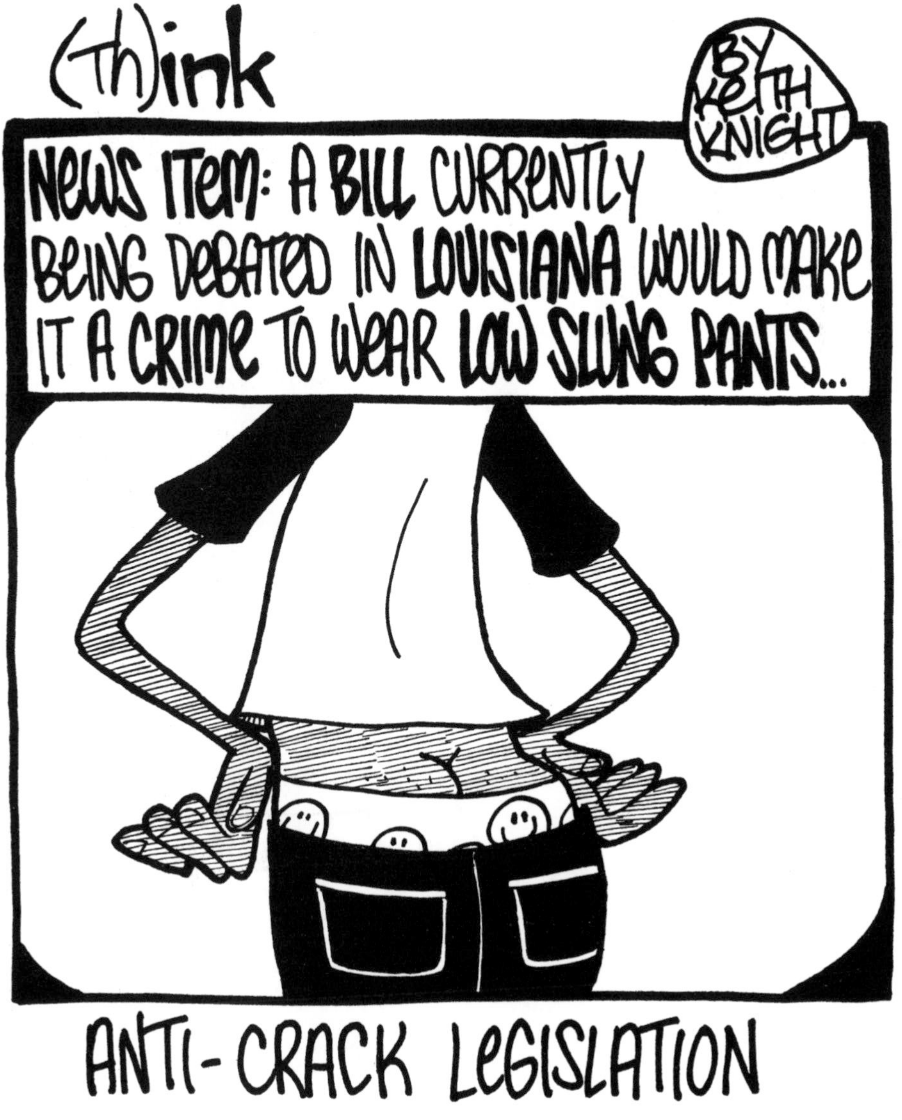

(TH)INK
BY KEITH KNIGHT
NEWS ITEM: A BILL CURRENTLY BEING DEBATED IN LOUISIANA WOULD MAKE IT A CRIME TO WEAR LOW SLUNG PANTS...
ANTI-CRACK LEGISLATION

(Th)ink
BY KEITH KNIGHT
BLACK PEOPLE DID IT!!
ROSEWOOD 1923
Black people did it!!
CHARLES STUART 1989
Black people did it!!
SUSAN SMITH 1994
A Mexican & a white lady did it!!
JENNIFER WILBANKS 2005
WHO SEZ BLACK FOLKS AIN'T MAKING PROGRESS?

(Th)ink
BY KEITH KNIGHT
NEWS ITEM: MORE BLACK-OWNED COFFEEHOUSES ARE POPPING UP IN NEIGHBORHOODS ACROSS THE COUNTRY...
excuse me... can I get more cream in this?
SELLOUT!!

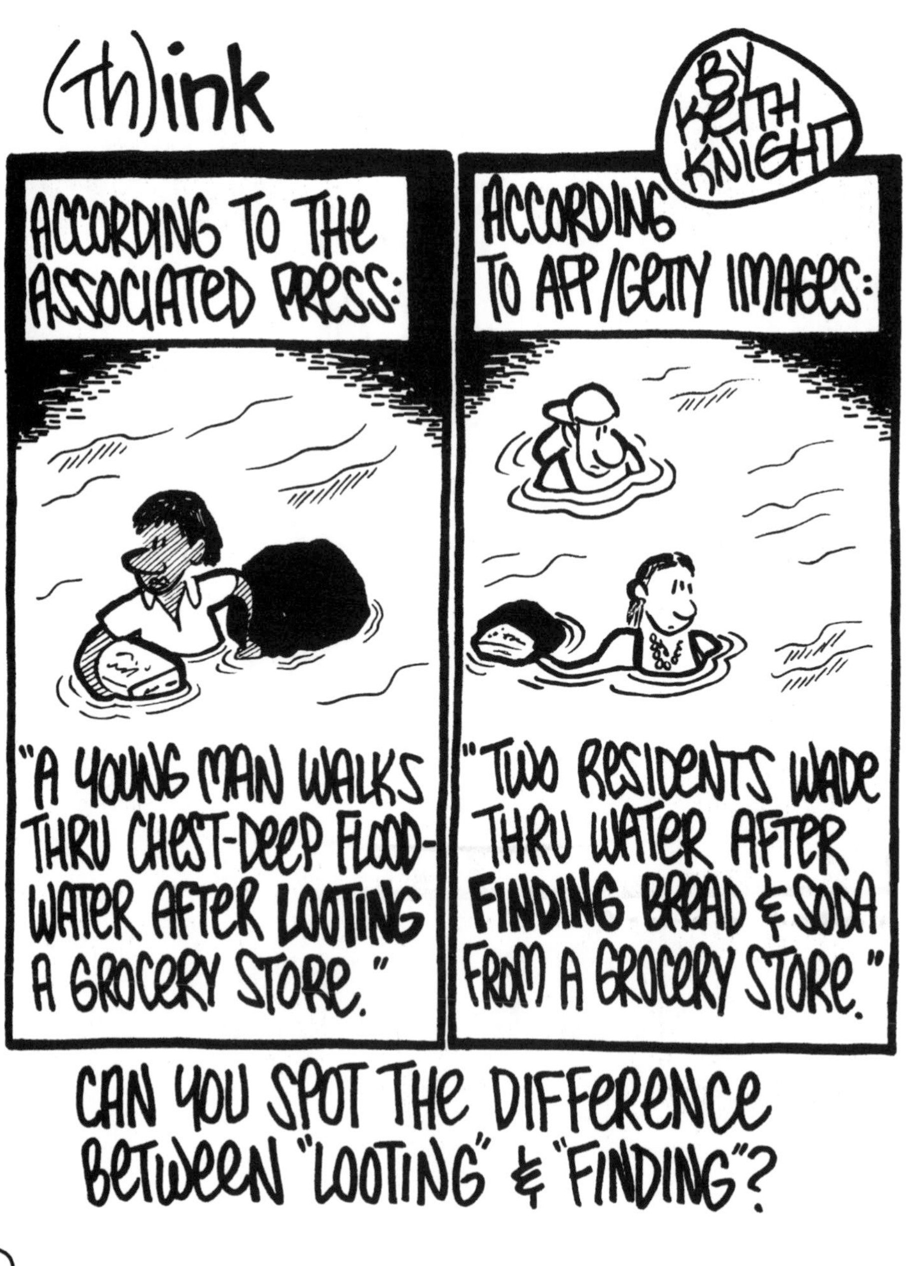
(TH)INK
BY KEITH KNIGHT
ACCORDING TO THE ASSOCIATED PRESS:
"A YOUNG MAN WALKS THRU CHEST-DEEP FLOOD-WATER AFTER LOOTING A GROCERY STORE."
ACCORDING TO AFP/GETTY IMAGES:
"TWO RESIDENTS WADE THRU WATER AFTER FINDING BREAD & SODA FROM A GROCERY STORE."
CAN YOU SPOT THE DIFFERENCE BETWEEN "LOOTING" & "FINDING"?

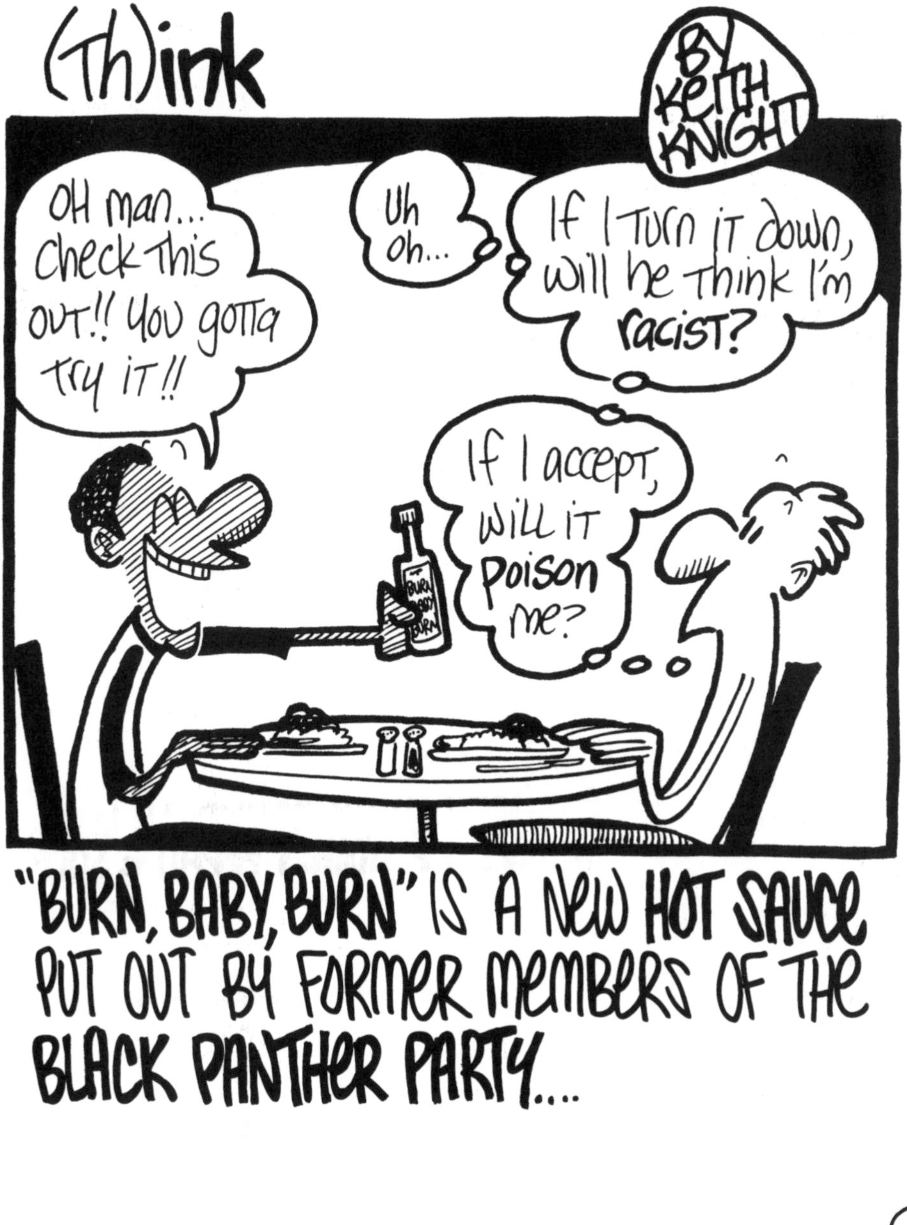
(Th)ink
BY KEITH KNIGHT
OH man... Check This OUT!! You gotta try IT!!
Uh oh...
If I Turn IT down, will he Think I'm racist?
If I accept, will IT poison me?
BURN BABY BURN
"BURN, BABY, BURN" IS A NEW HOT SAUCE PUT OUT BY FORMER MEMBERS OF THE BLACK PANTHER PARTY....

(Th)ink
BY KEITH KNIGHT
THEY'RE ROLLING BACK THEIR PRICES TO 1992!
IT'S PRACTICALLY LOOTING ALL OVER AGAIN!!
BURGER KING
RODNEY KING & REGINALD DENNY SAY:
DENNY'S
You can beat us, but you cannot beat these prices!!
Now with more black & asian employees!!
Mack

(Th)ink

BY KEITH KNIGHT

I believe The **key** to accumulating **wealth** & financial success is To have a **diverse** & **active** portfolio...

That's why I play the **scratch** cards...

..The **Daily** & **Weekly** numbers..

..AND CHURCH BINGO!!

ACCORDING TO A RECENT SURVEY, MINORITIES EXPRESSED **HIGHER CONFIDENCE** IN BUILDING **WEALTH** VIA **THE LOTTERY** ABOVE SAVINGS & RETIREMENT PLANNING....

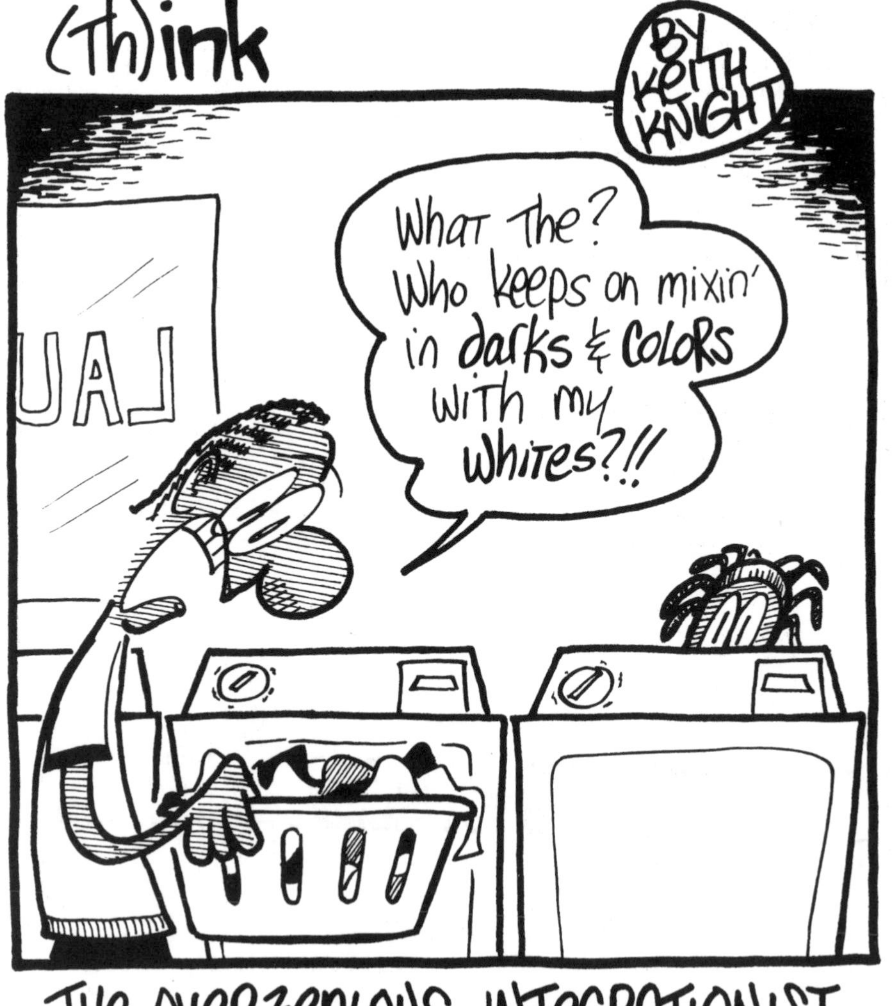
(Th)ink
BY KEITH KNIGHT
What The? Who keeps on mixin' in darks & COLORS with my whites?!!
UAL
THE OVERZEALOUS INTEGRATIONIST STRIKES AGAIN

(Th)ink
BY KEITH KNIGHT
NEWS ITEM: MEXICAN POSTAL OFFICIALS DEFEND THEIR DECISION TO DISTRIBUTE STAMPS CELEBRATING A BUG-EYED, BIG-LIPPED, BLACK CARTOON CHARACTER CALLED MEMIN PINGUIN...
I think somebody in the office mentioned that it might be offensive...
TEQUILA
..but we were just too lazy to stop it...

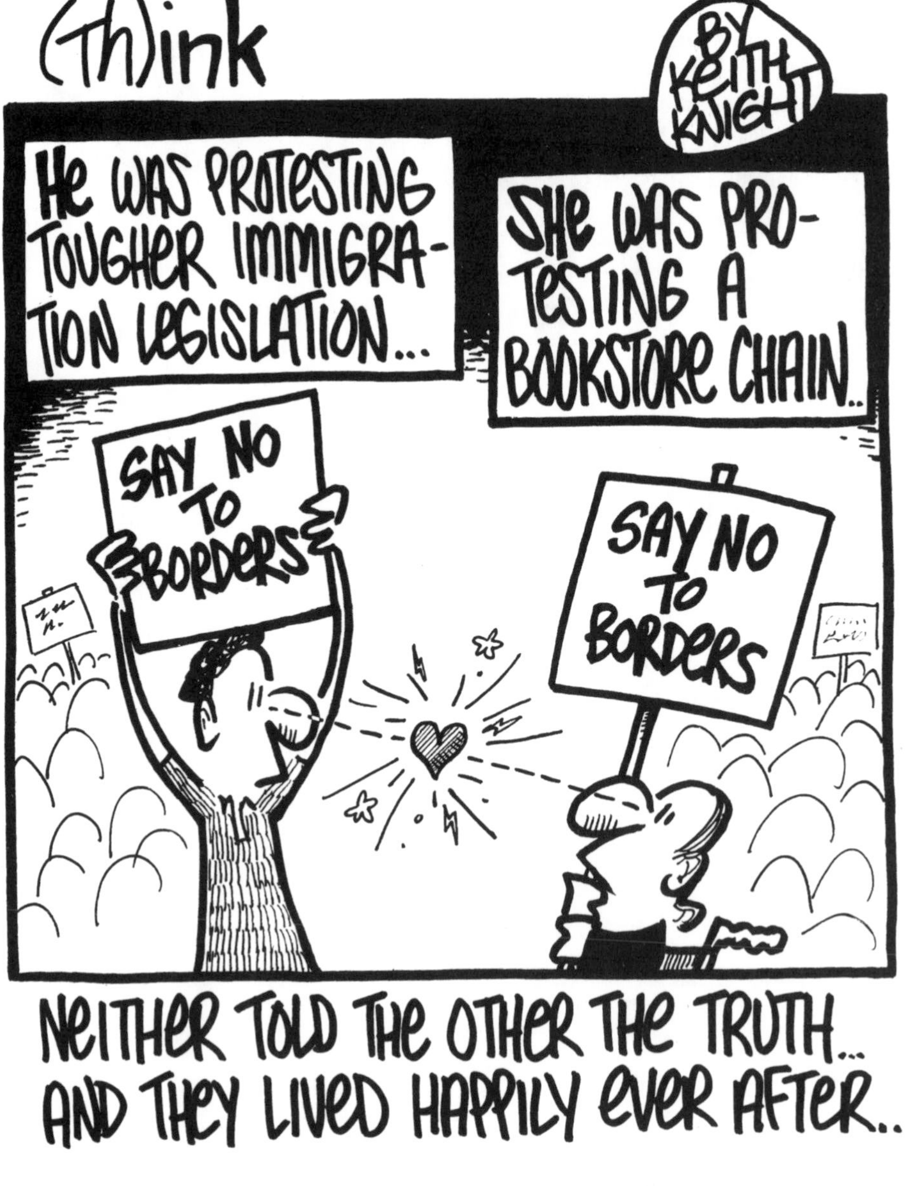

(TH)INK
BY KEITH KNIGHT
HE WAS PROTESTING TOUGHER IMMIGRATION LEGISLATION...
SHE WAS PROTESTING A BOOKSTORE CHAIN..
SAY NO TO BORDERS
SAY NO TO BORDERS
NEITHER TOLD THE OTHER THE TRUTH...
AND THEY LIVED HAPPILY EVER AFTER..

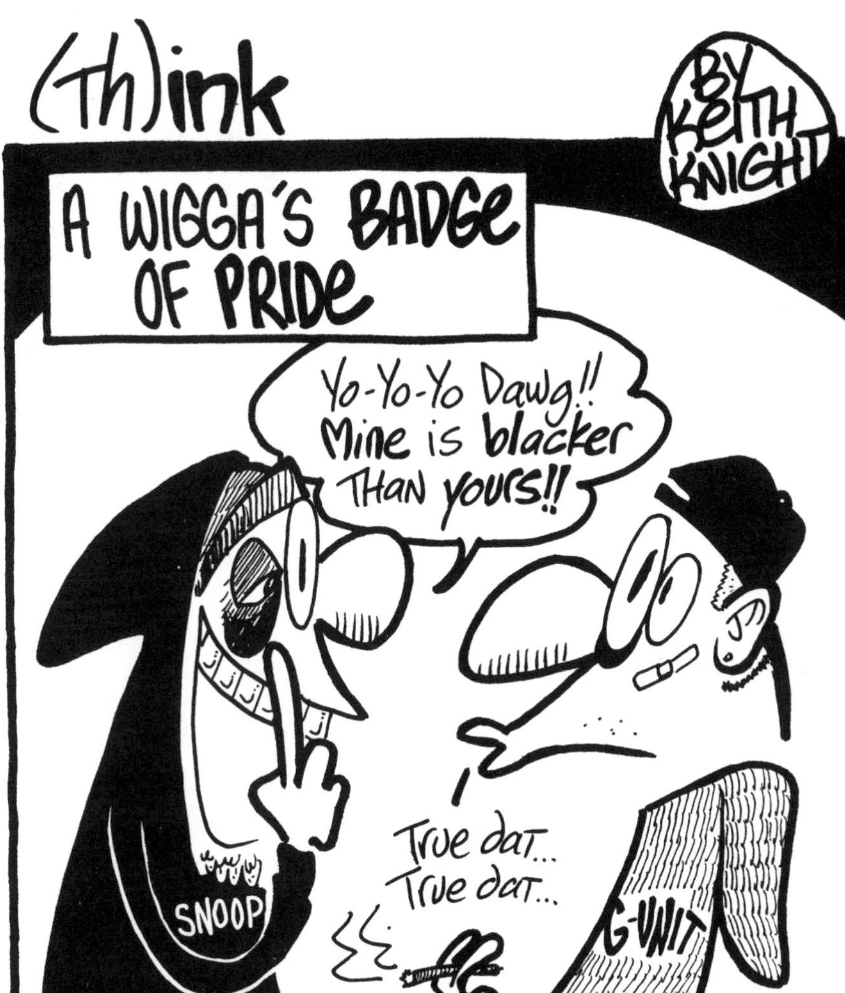
(TH)INK
BY KEITH KNIGHT
A WIGGA'S BADGE OF PRIDE
Yo-Yo-Yo Dawg!! Mine is blacker THAN yours!!
True dat... True dat...
SNOOP
G-UNIT

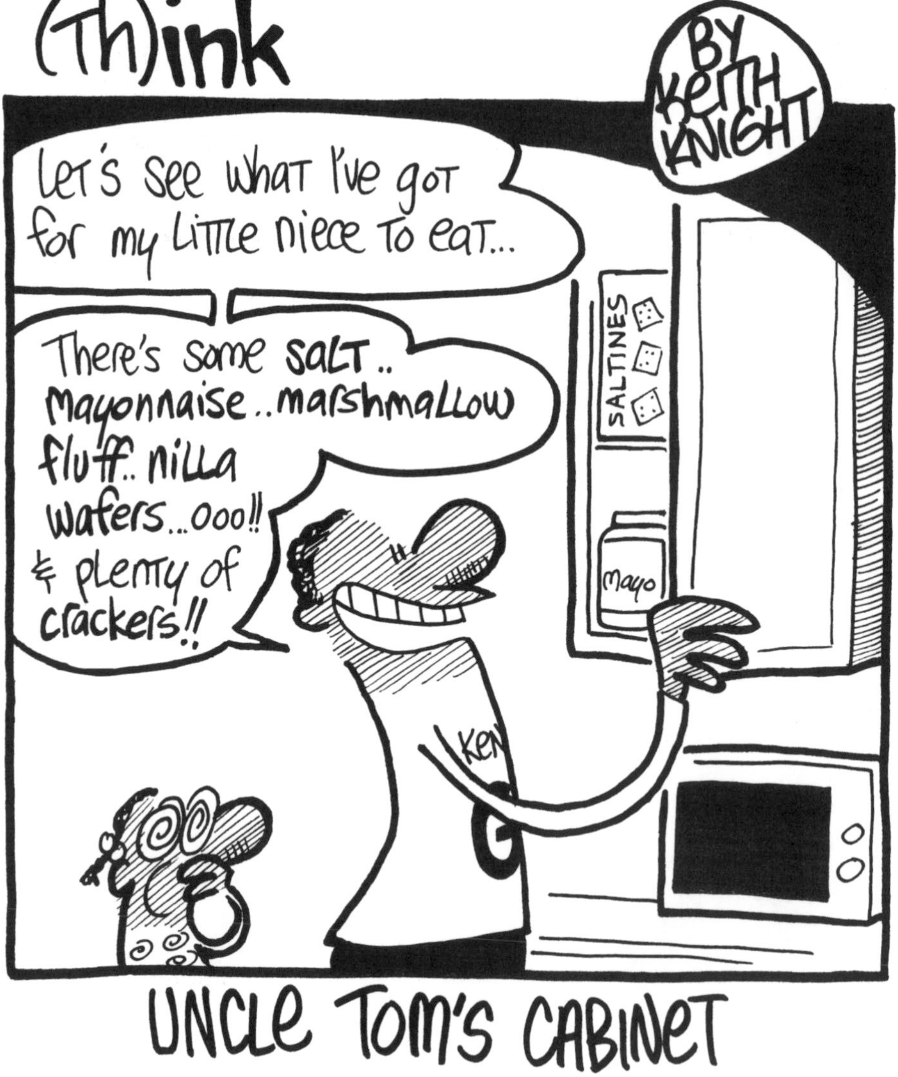
(Th)ink
BY KEITH KNIGHT
let's see what I've got for my little niece to eat...
There's some SALT.. mayonnaise..marshmallow fluff.. nilla wafers...ooo!! & plenty of crackers!!
SALTINES
mayo
KEN

UNCLE TOM'S CABINET

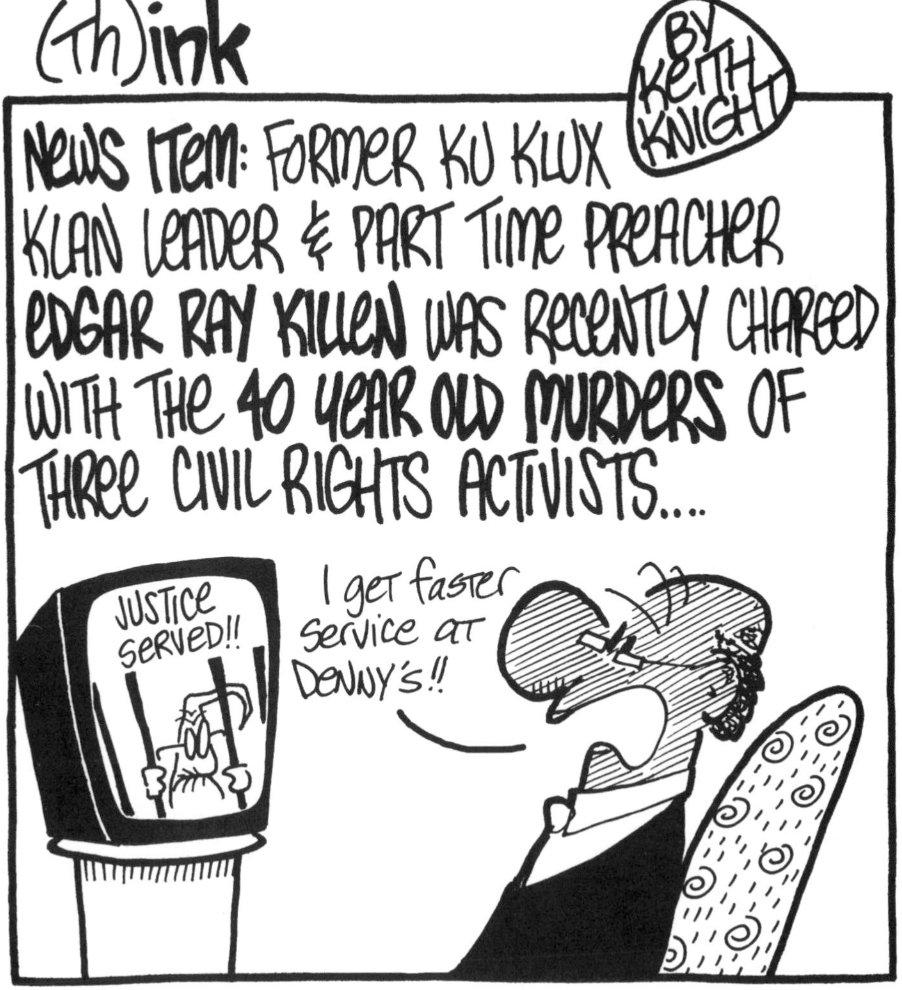
(TH)INK
BY KEITH KNIGHT
NEWS ITEM: FORMER KU KLUX KLAN LEADER & PART TIME PREACHER EDGAR RAY KILLEN WAS RECENTLY CHARGED WITH THE 40 YEAR OLD MURDERS OF THREE CIVIL RIGHTS ACTIVISTS....
JUSTICE SERVED!!
I get faster service at DENNY'S!!

(Th)ink
BY KEITH KNIGHT
"PEOPLE ALWAYS SAY THAT I DIDN'T GIVE UP MY SEAT BECAUSE I WAS TIRED, BUT THAT WASN'T TRUE..."
"..THE ONLY TIRED I WAS, WAS TIRED OF GIVING IN."
ROSA PARKS
1913-2005

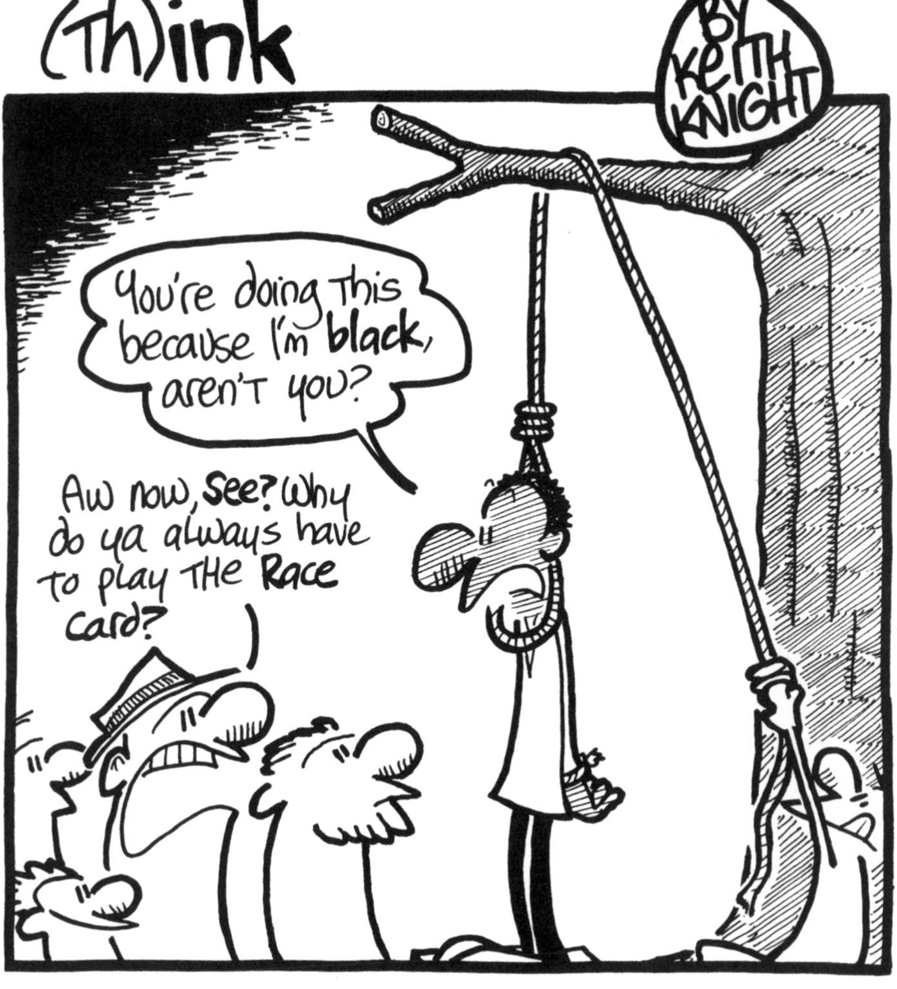
(Th)ink
BY KEITH KNIGHT
You're doing this because I'm black, aren't you?
Aw now, see? Why do ya always have to play the race card?

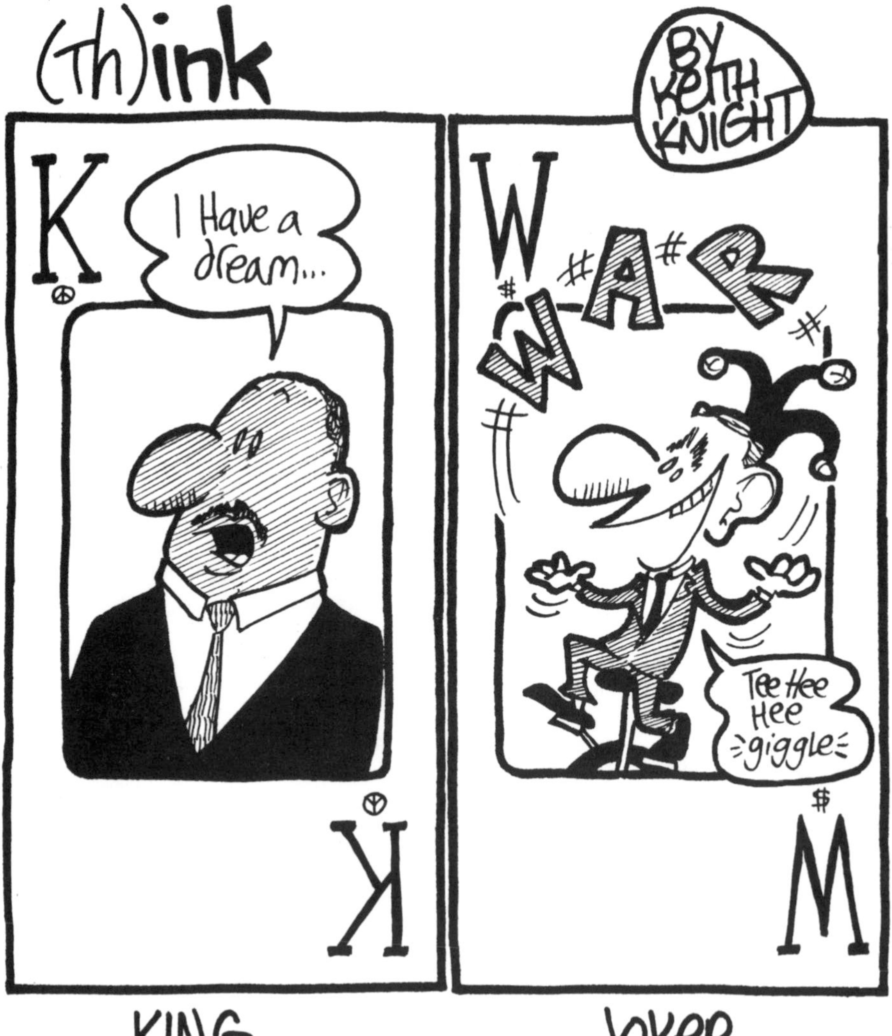
(th)ink
BY KEITH KNIGHT
K
I Have a dream...
K
KING
W
WAR
Tee Hee Hee giggle
M
JOKER

(Th)ink
BY KEITH KNIGHT
MARTIN LUTHER KING BLVD.
ANYTOWN, U.S.A.
LIQUOR
LOTTO
CHECK-CASHING
I HAVE A NIGHTMARE

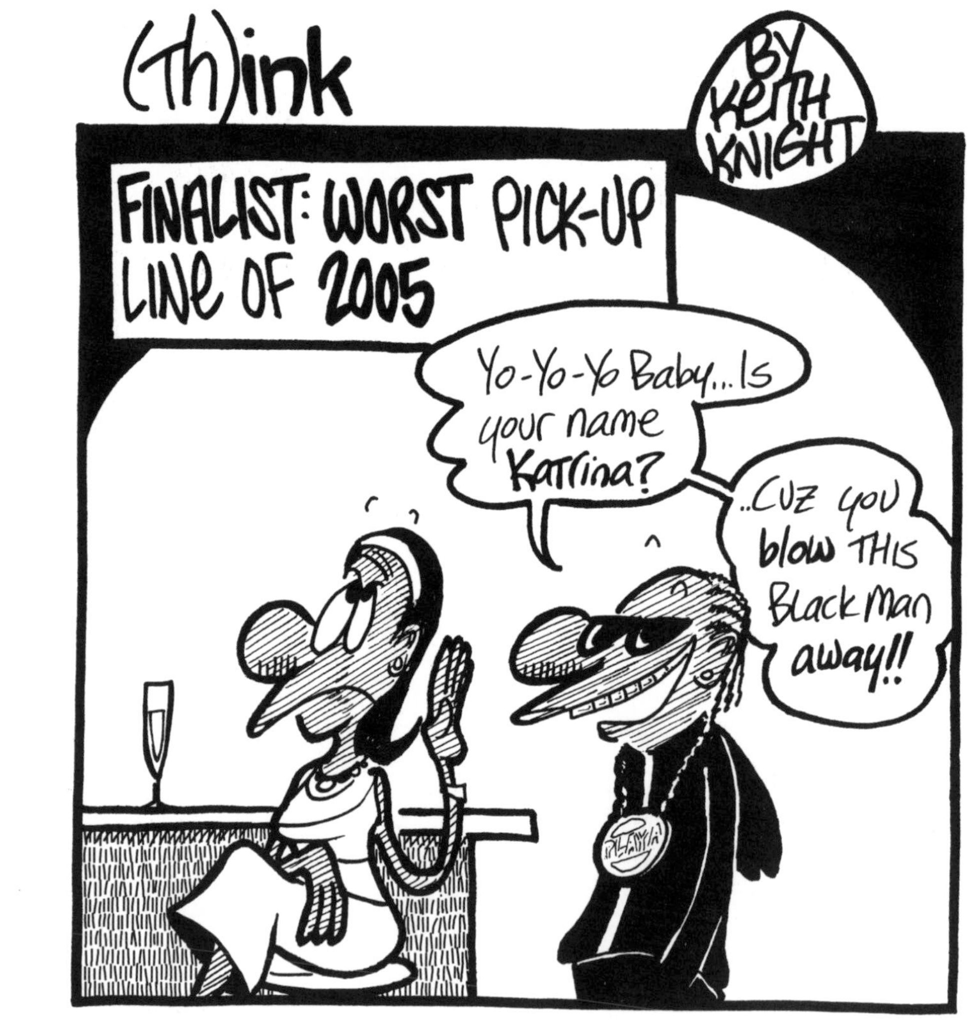
(Th)ink
BY KEITH KNIGHT
FINALIST: WORST PICK-UP LINE OF 2005
Yo-Yo-Yo Baby... Is your name Katrina?
..CUZ you blow THIS Black Man away!!

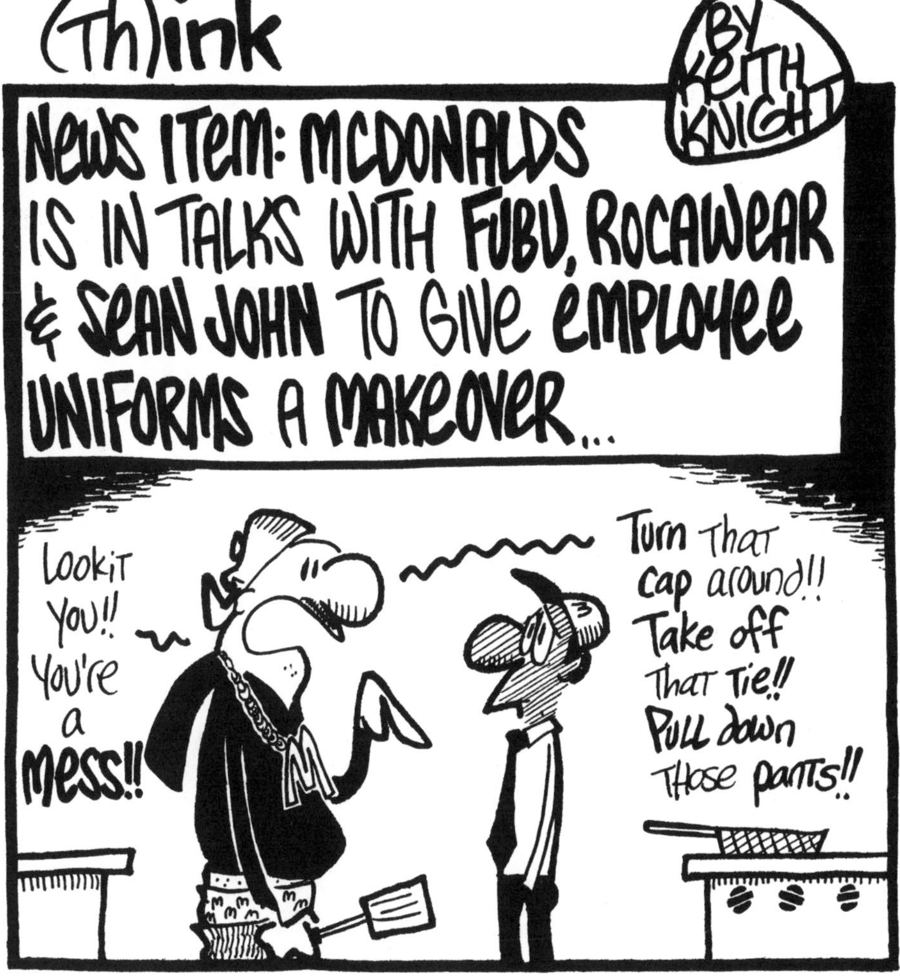
(Th)ink
By Keith Knight
News Item: McDonalds is in talks with FUBU, Rocawear & Sean John to give employee uniforms a makeover...
Lookit you!! You're a mess!!
Turn that cap around!! Take off that tie!! Pull down those pants!!

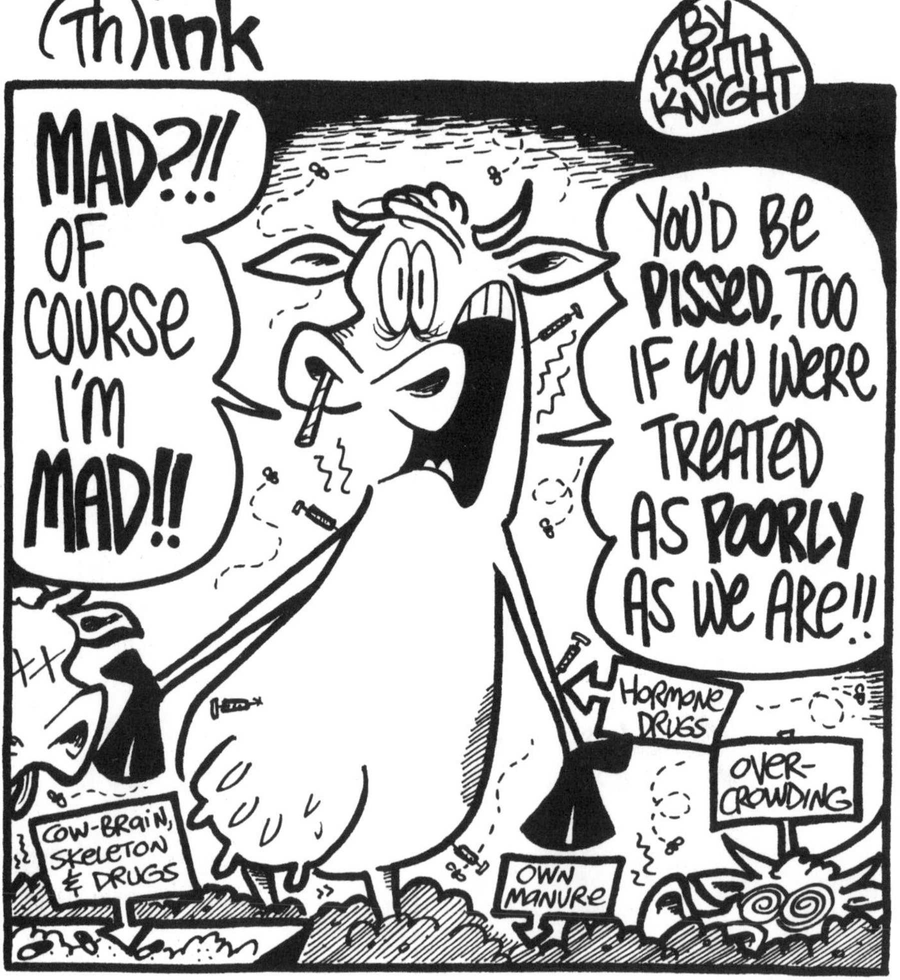
(Th)ink
BY KEITH KNIGHT
MAD?!! OF COURSE I'M MAD!!
YOU'D BE PISSED, TOO IF YOU WERE TREATED AS POORLY AS WE ARE!!
COW-BRAIN, SKELETON & DRUGS
HORMONE DRUGS
OVER-CROWDING
OWN MANURE

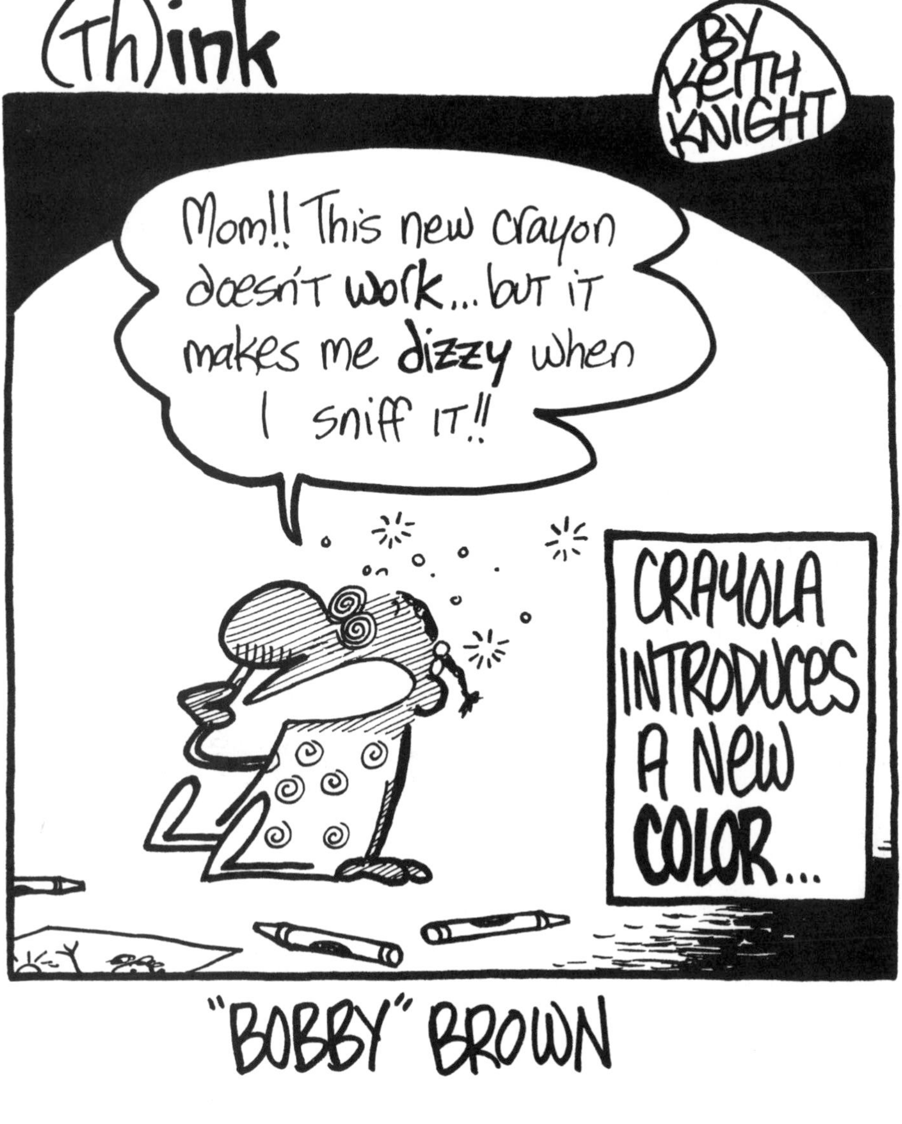
(Th)ink
BY KEITH KNIGHT
Mom!! This new crayon doesn't work... but it makes me dizzy when I sniff it!!
CRAYOLA INTRODUCES A NEW COLOR...
"BOBBY" BROWN

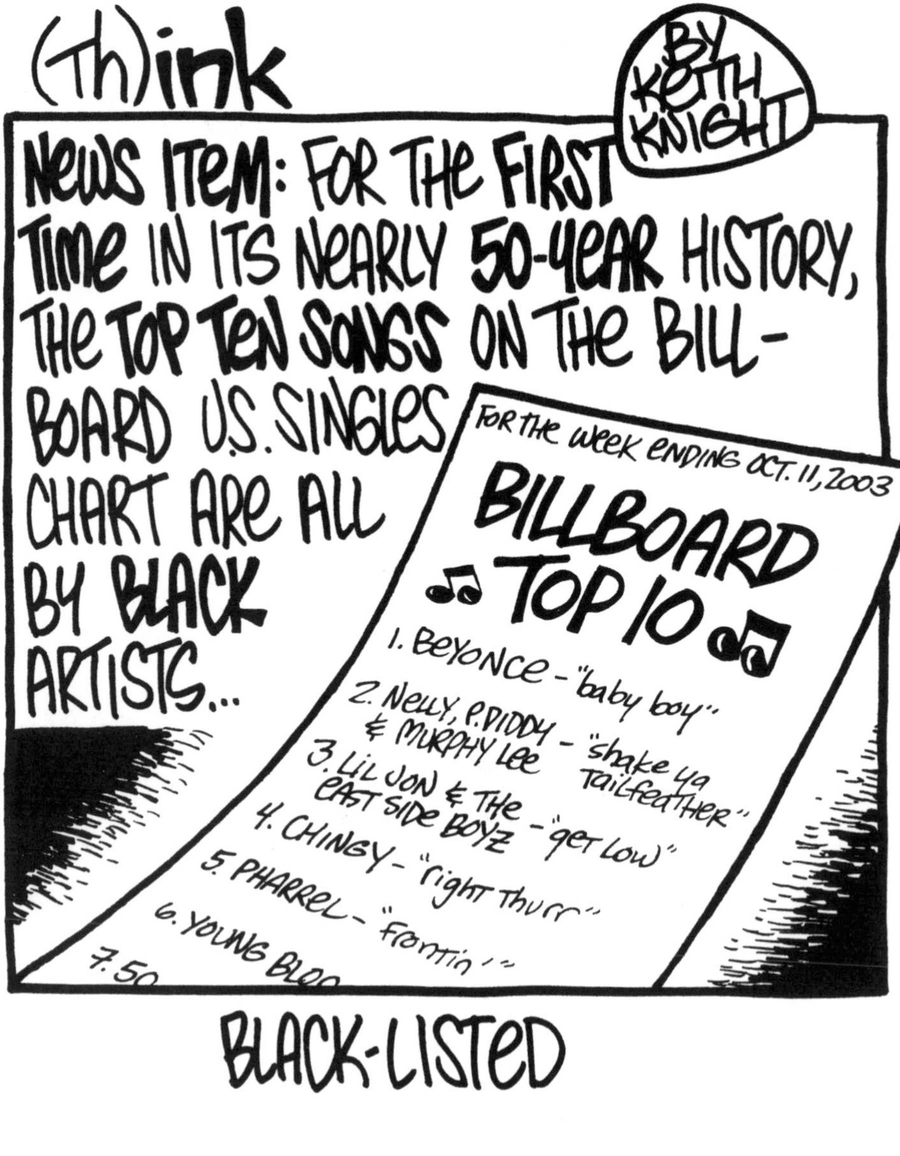

(Th)ink
BY KEITH KNIGHT
NEWS ITEM: FOR THE FIRST TIME IN ITS NEARLY 50-YEAR HISTORY, THE TOP TEN SONGS ON THE BILL-BOARD U.S. SINGLES CHART ARE ALL BY BLACK ARTISTS...
FOR THE WEEK ENDING OCT. 11, 2003
BILLBOARD TOP 10
1. BEYONCE - "baby boy"
2. NELLY, P.DIDDY & MURPHY LEE - "shake ya Tailfeather"
3. LIL JON & THE EAST SIDE BOYZ - "get low"
4. CHINGY - "right thurr"
5. PHARREL - "frontin'"
6. YOUNG BLOO
7. 50
BLACK-LISTED

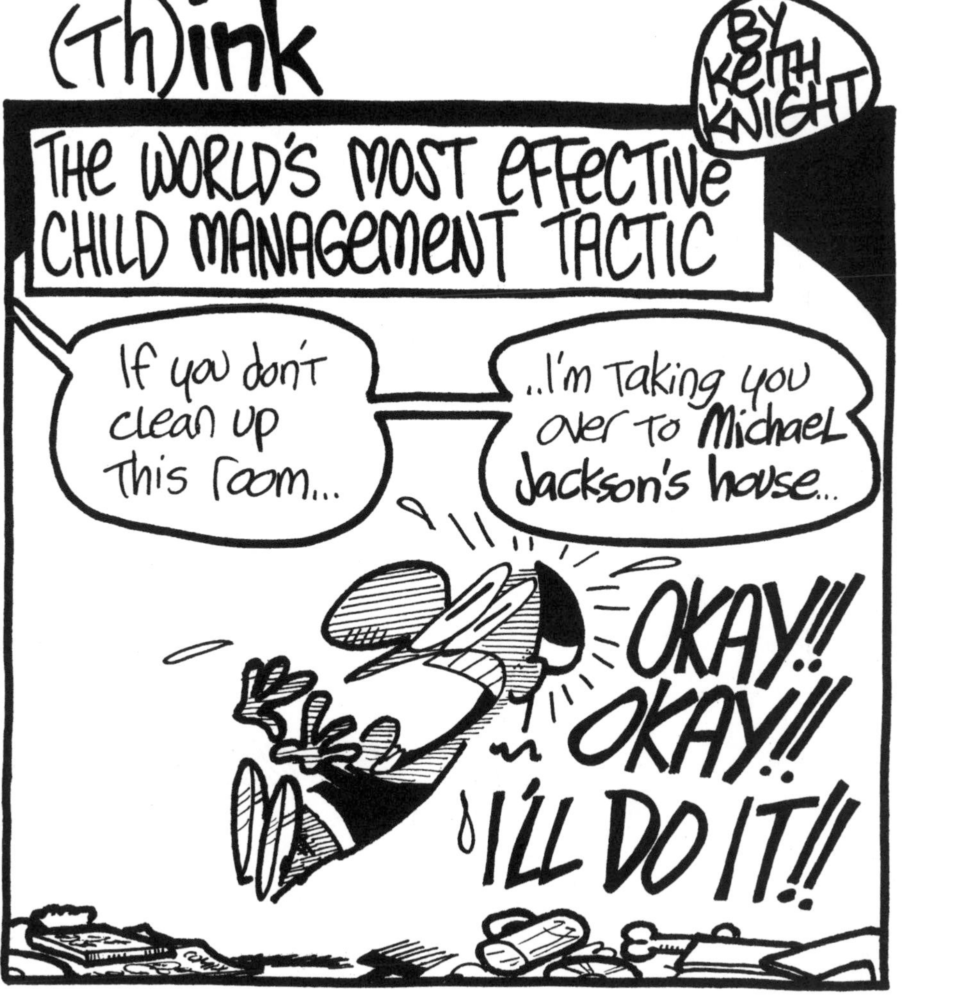
(Th)ink
BY KEITH KNIGHT
THE WORLD'S MOST EFFECTIVE CHILD MANAGEMENT TACTIC
If you don't clean up this room...
..I'm Taking you over to Michael Jackson's house...
OKAY!! OKAY!! I'LL DO IT!!

WHY THE RHODE ISLAND NITECLUB TRAGEDY WOULD'VE BEEN EVEN WORSE HAD IT BEEN A BLACK AUDIENCE IN ATTENDANCE...

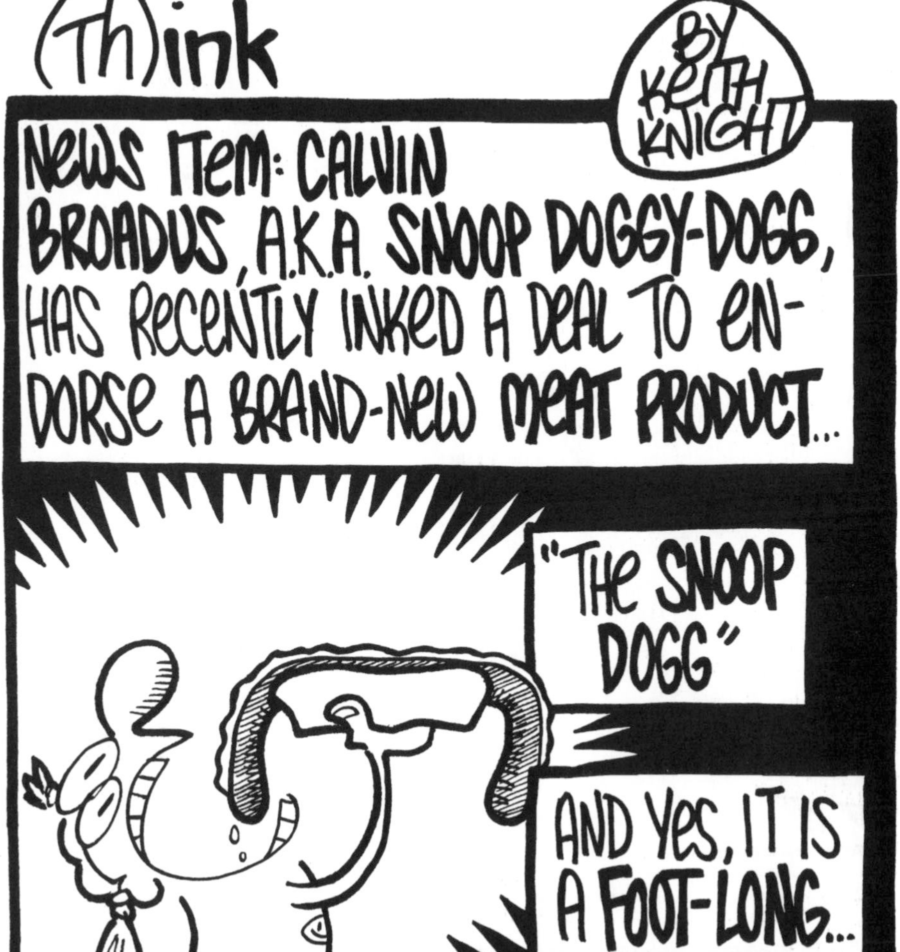
(Th)ink
BY KEITH KNIGHT
NEWS ITEM: CALVIN BROADUS, A.K.A. SNOOP DOGGY-DOGG, HAS RECENTLY INKED A DEAL TO ENDORSE A BRAND-NEW MEAT PRODUCT...
"THE SNOOP DOGG"
AND YES, IT IS A FOOT-LONG...

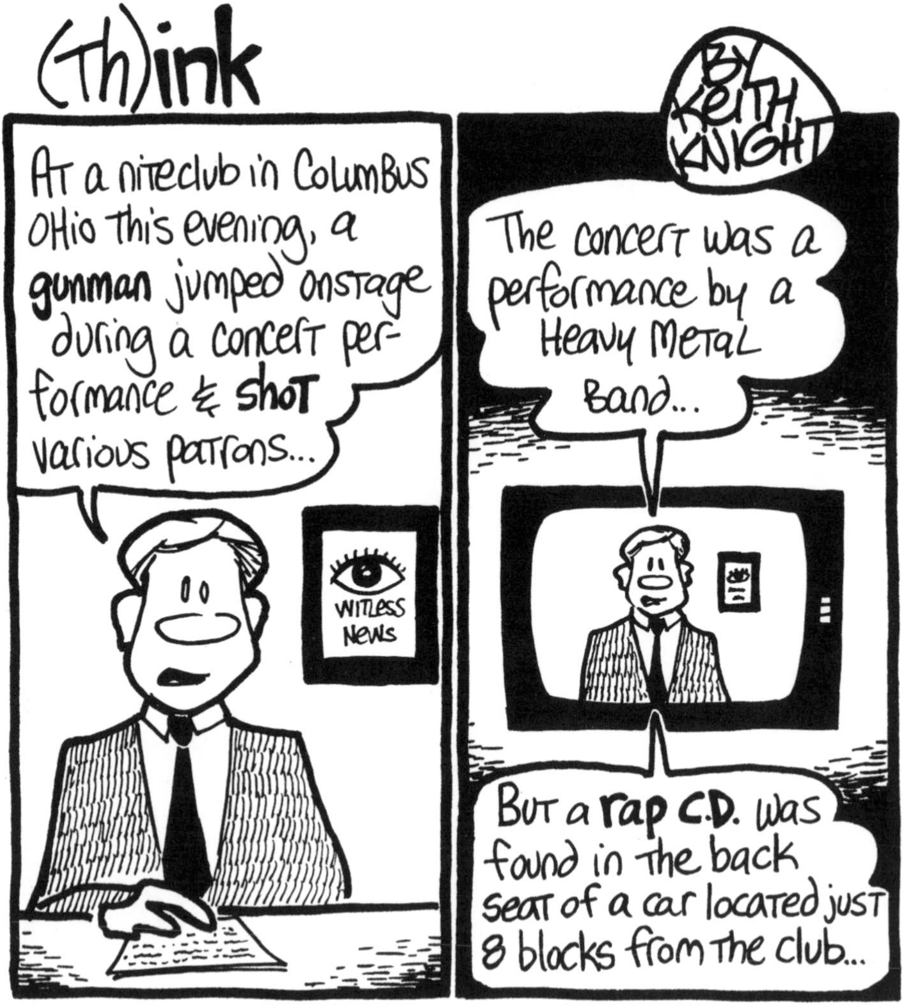
(Th)ink
By Keith Knight
At a niteclub in Columbus Ohio this evening, a gunman jumped onstage during a concert performance & shot various patrons...
Witless News
The concert was a performance by a Heavy Metal Band...
But a rap C.D. was found in the back seat of a car located just 8 blocks from the club...

(Th)ink
BY KEITH KNIGHT
IN 1989, A XEROX SALESMAN NAMED MATTHEW KNOWLES PUT TOGETHER A SINGING GROUP THAT INCLUDED HIS DAUGHTER BEYONCE & KELLY ROWLAND...
I'm a survivor...
HE RECENTLY SOLD HIS MUSIC COMPANY FOR TEN MILLION DOLLARS..
FATHER KNOWLES BEST

(Th)ink

BY KEITH KNIGHT

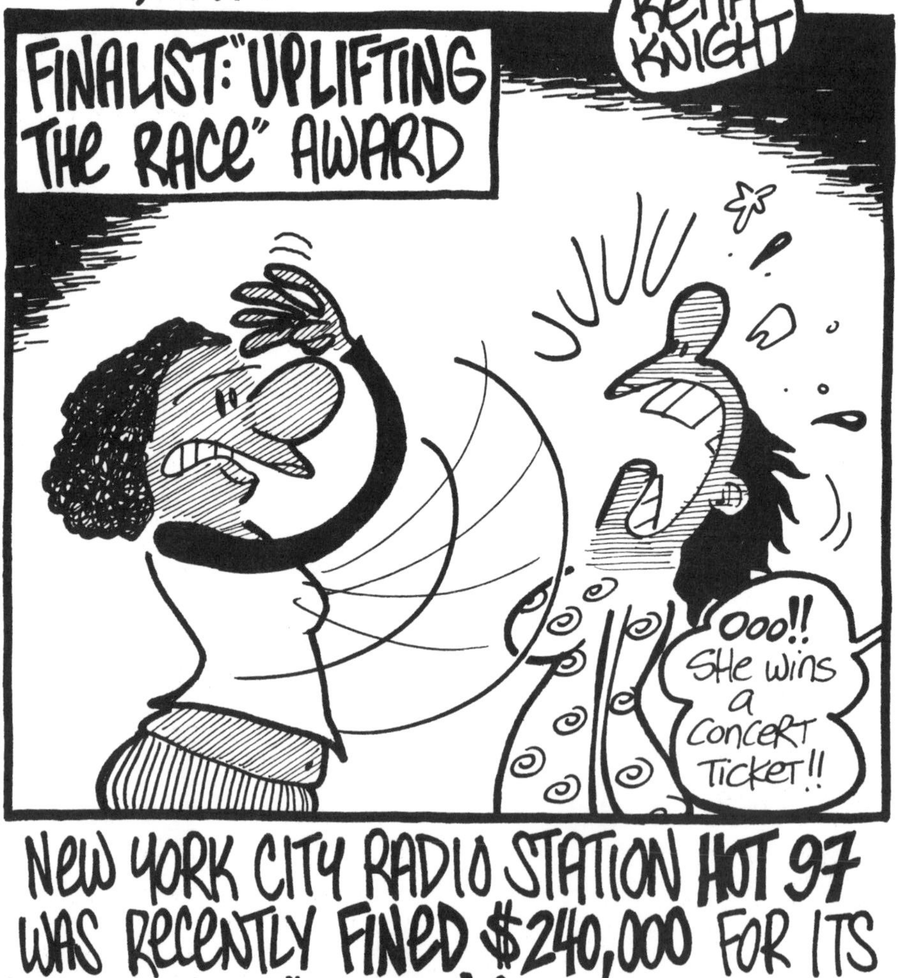
FINALIST: "UPLIFTING THE RACE" AWARD
Ooo!! SHE wins a CONCERT TICKET!!

NEW YORK CITY RADIO STATION **HOT 97** WAS RECENTLY **FINED $240,000** FOR ITS **"SMACKFEST" SLAPPING** CONTESTS...

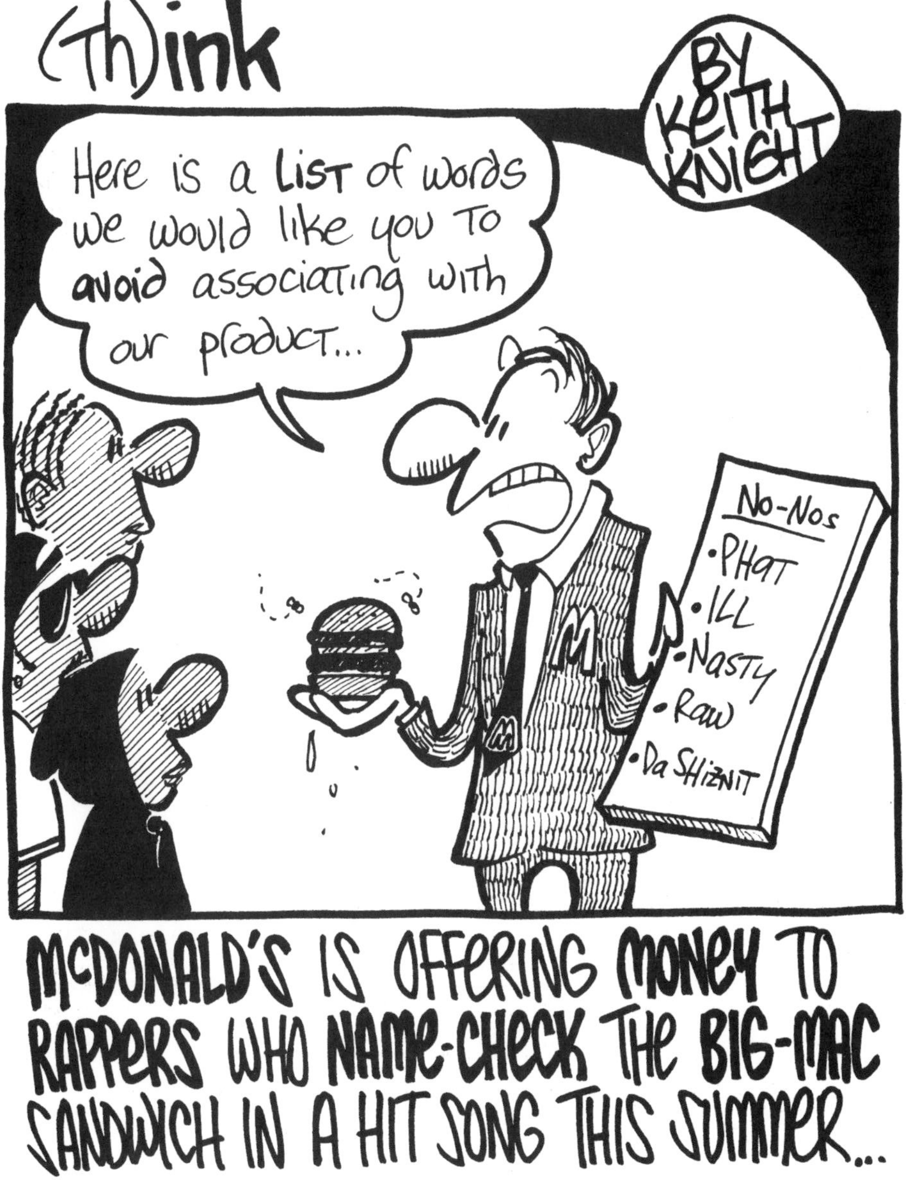
(Th)ink
BY KEITH KNIGHT
Here is a LIST of words we would like you to avoid associating with our product...
No-Nos
•PHAT
•ILL
•NASTY
•Raw
•Da SHIZNIT
McDONALD'S IS OFFERING MONEY TO RAPPERS WHO NAME-CHECK THE BIG-MAC SANDWICH IN A HIT SONG THIS SUMMER...

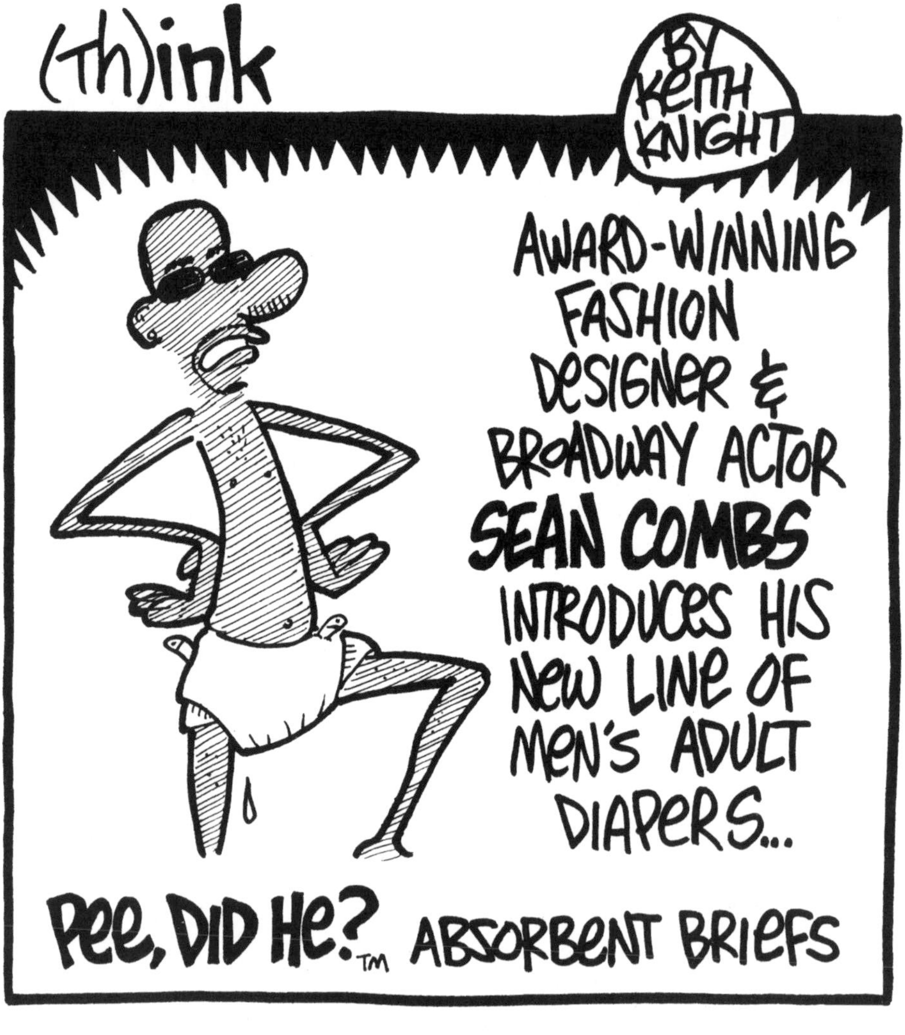
(th)ink
BY KEITH KNIGHT
AWARD-WINNING FASHION DESIGNER & BROADWAY ACTOR SEAN COMBS INTRODUCES HIS NEW LINE OF MEN'S ADULT DIAPERS...
PEE, DID HE?™ ABSORBENT BRIEFS

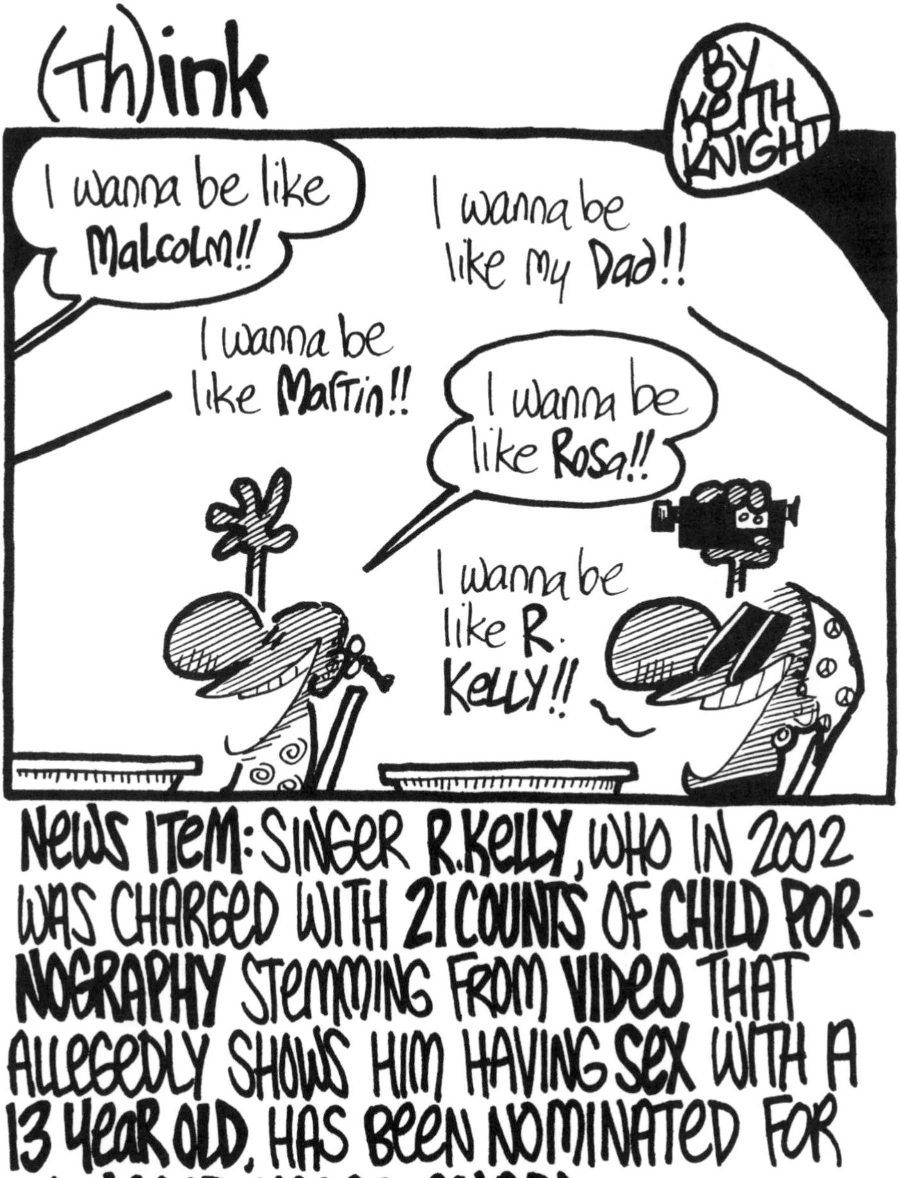
(Th)ink
BY KEITH KNIGHT
I wanna be like Malcolm!!
I wanna be like my Dad!!
I wanna be like Martin!!
I wanna be like Rosa!!
I wanna be like R. Kelly!!

NEWS ITEM: SINGER R. KELLY, WHO IN 2002 WAS CHARGED WITH 21 COUNTS OF CHILD PORNOGRAPHY STEMMING FROM VIDEO THAT ALLEGEDLY SHOWS HIM HAVING SEX WITH A 13 YEAR OLD, HAS BEEN NOMINATED FOR AN NAACP IMAGE AWARD...

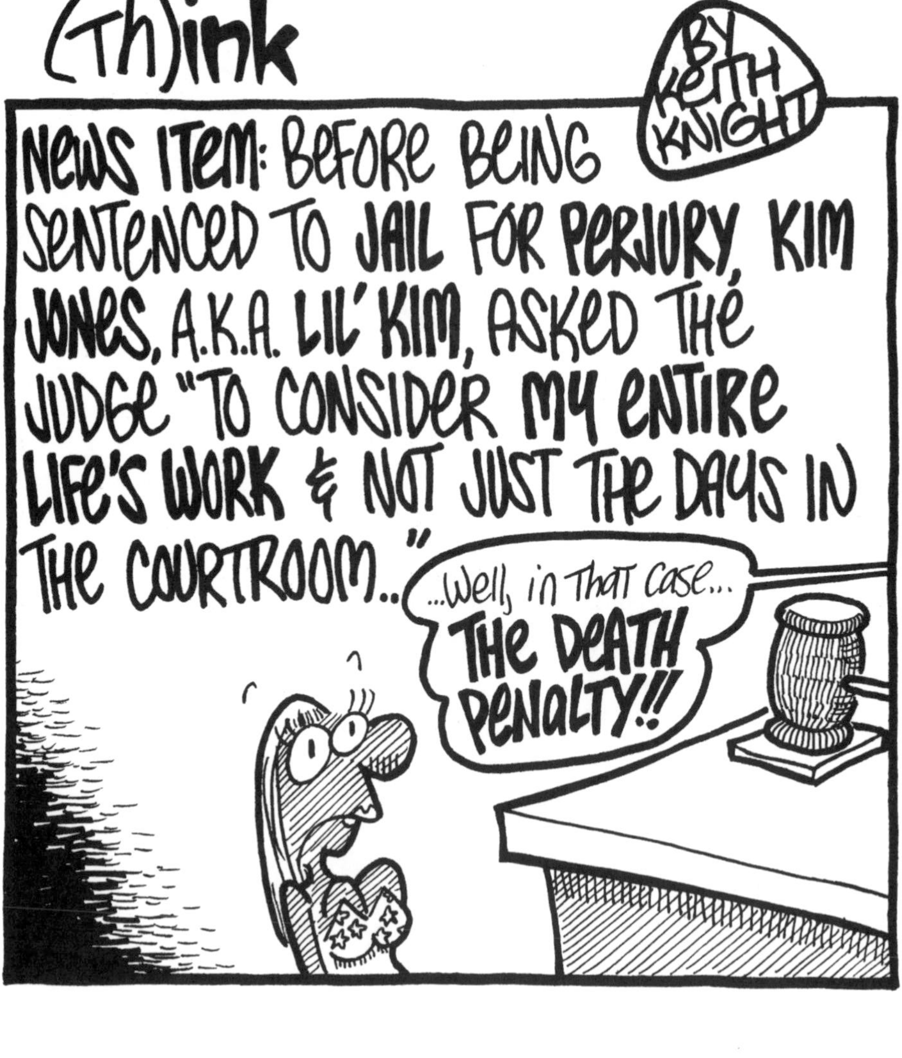
(TH)INK
BY KEITH KNIGHT
NEWS ITEM: BEFORE BEING SENTENCED TO JAIL FOR PERJURY, KIM JONES, A.K.A. LIL' KIM, ASKED THE JUDGE "TO CONSIDER MY ENTIRE LIFE'S WORK & NOT JUST THE DAYS IN THE COURTROOM..."
...WELL, IN THAT CASE... THE DEATH PENALTY!!

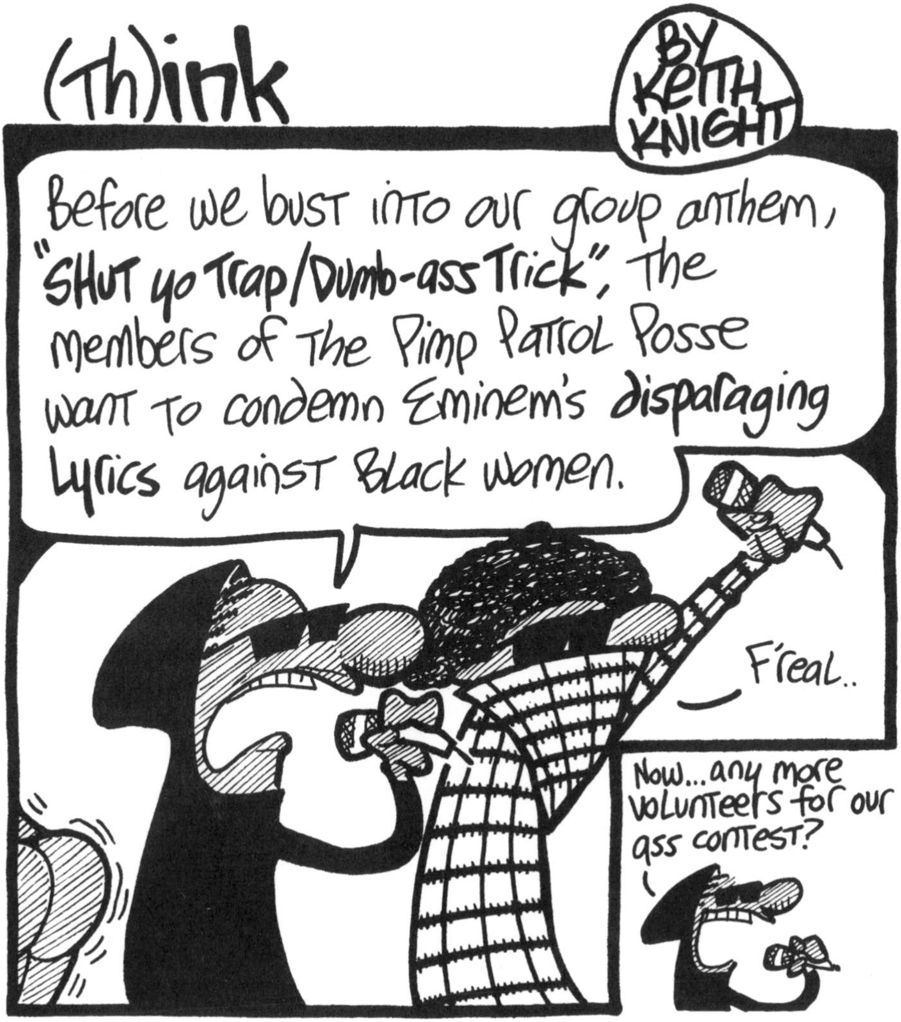
(Th)ink
BY KEITH KNIGHT
Before we bust into our group anthem, "SHUT yo Trap/Dumb-ass Trick", the members of the Pimp Patrol Posse want to condemn Eminem's disparaging lyrics against Black women.
F'real..
Now...any more volunteers for our ass contest?

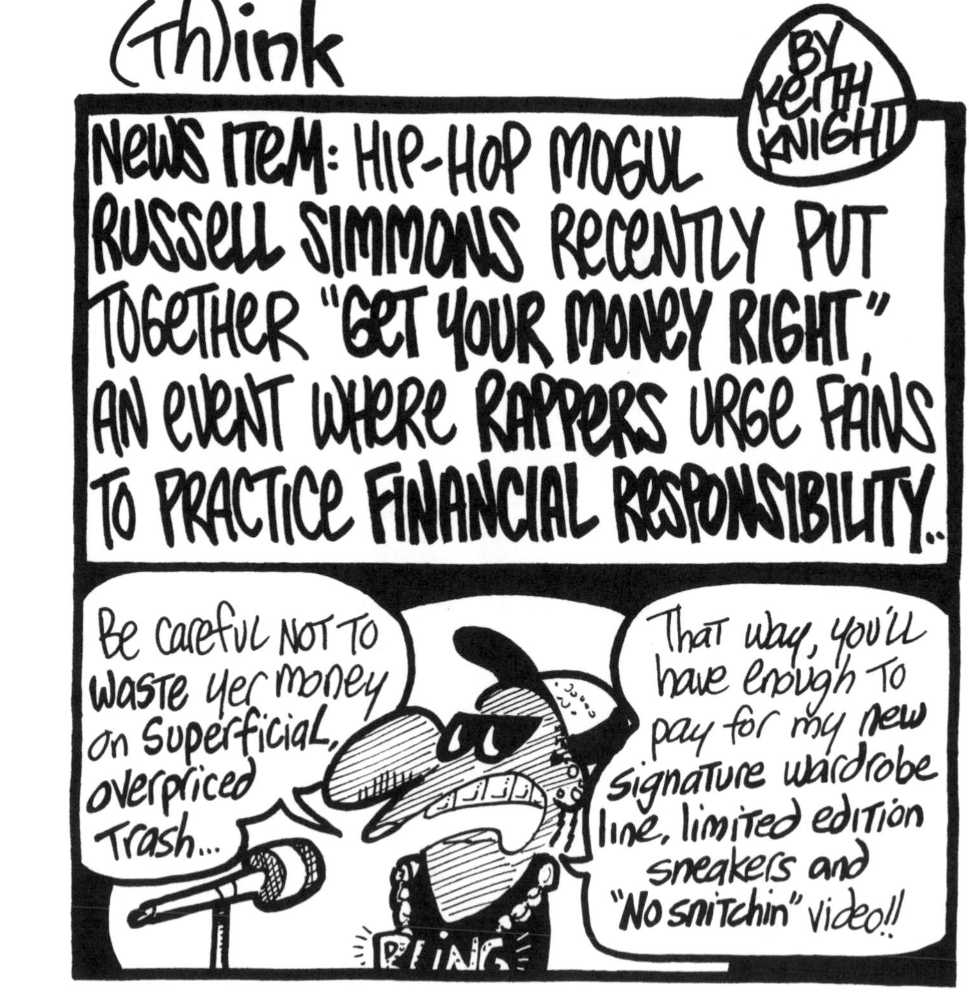
(TH)ink
BY KEITH KNIGHT
NEWS ITEM: HIP-HOP MOGUL RUSSELL SIMMONS RECENTLY PUT TOGETHER "GET YOUR MONEY RIGHT", AN EVENT WHERE RAPPERS URGE FANS TO PRACTICE FINANCIAL RESPONSIBILITY..
Be careful NOT TO waste yer money on Superficial, overpriced Trash...
That way, you'll have enough to pay for my new signature wardrobe line, limited edition sneakers and "No snitchin" video!!

(Th)ink
BY KEITH KNIGHT
ACCORDING TO THE NEW BOOK "ROOM FULL OF MIRRORS", GUITAR LEGEND JIMI HENDRIX PRETENDED TO BE GAY TO AVOID GOING TO VIETNAM...
..'Scuse me while I kiss This guy!!
HA!! I Told you That's what He's been singin'!!
ROOM FULL of MIRRORS
ROOM F...

(Th)ink

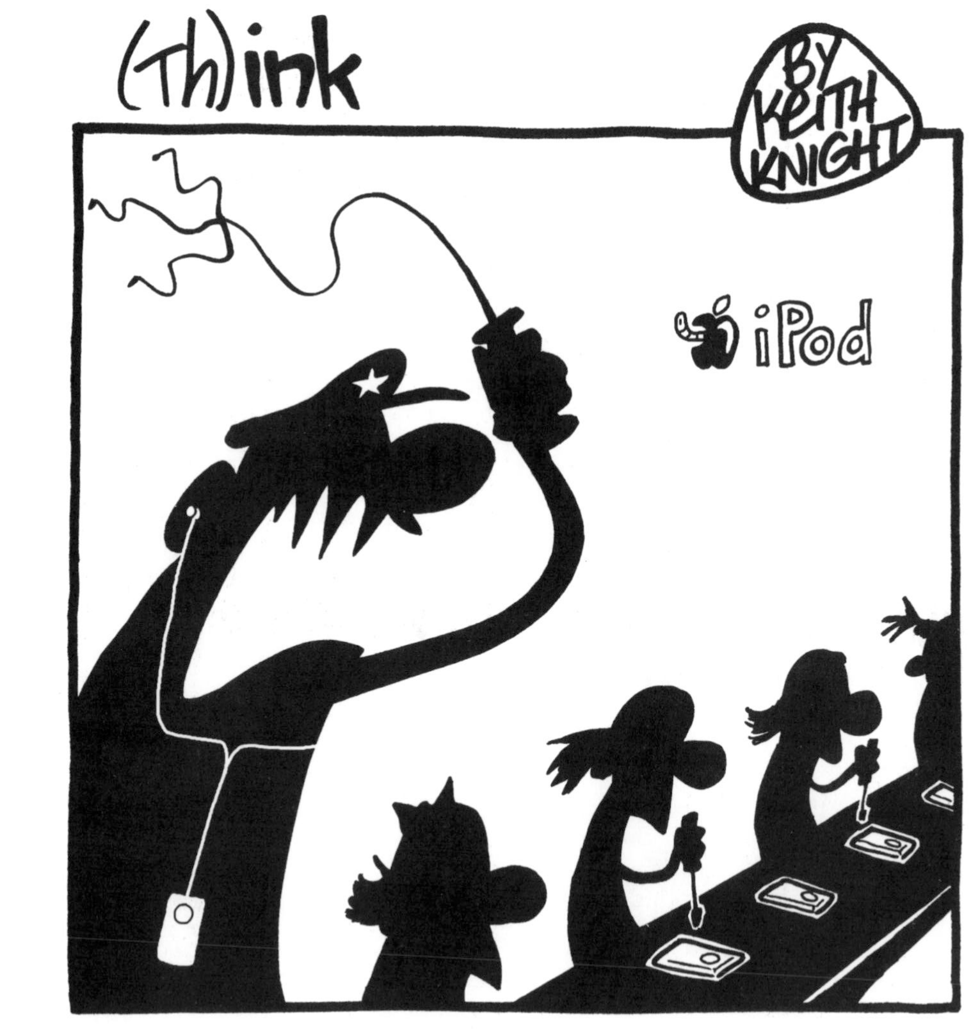
BY KEITH KNIGHT
iPod

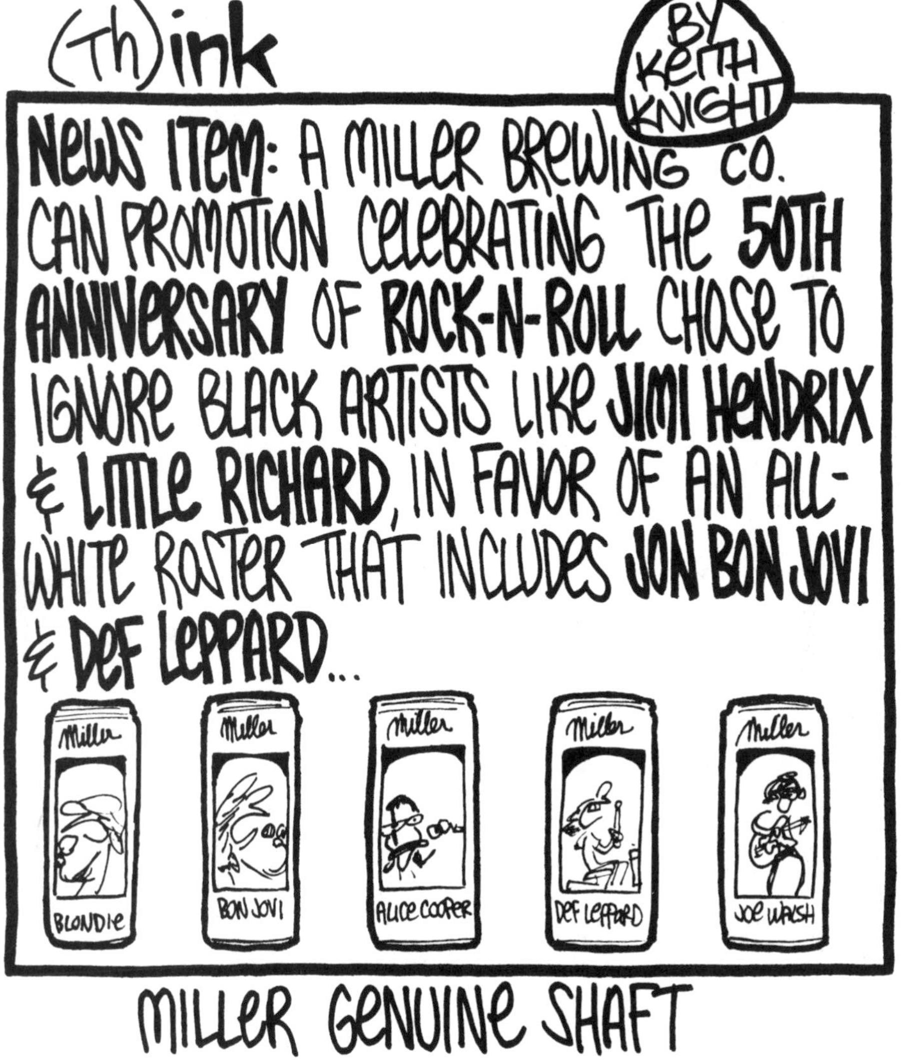
(Th)ink
BY KEITH KNIGHT
NEWS ITEM: A MILLER BREWING CO. CAN PROMOTION CELEBRATING THE 50TH ANNIVERSARY OF ROCK-N-ROLL CHOSE TO IGNORE BLACK ARTISTS LIKE JIMI HENDRIX & LITTLE RICHARD, IN FAVOR OF AN ALL-WHITE ROSTER THAT INCLUDES JON BON JOVI & DEF LEPPARD...
Miller
BLONDIE
Miller
BON JOVI
Miller
ALICE COOPER
Miller
DEF LEPPARD
Miller
JOE WALSH
MILLER GENUINE SHAFT

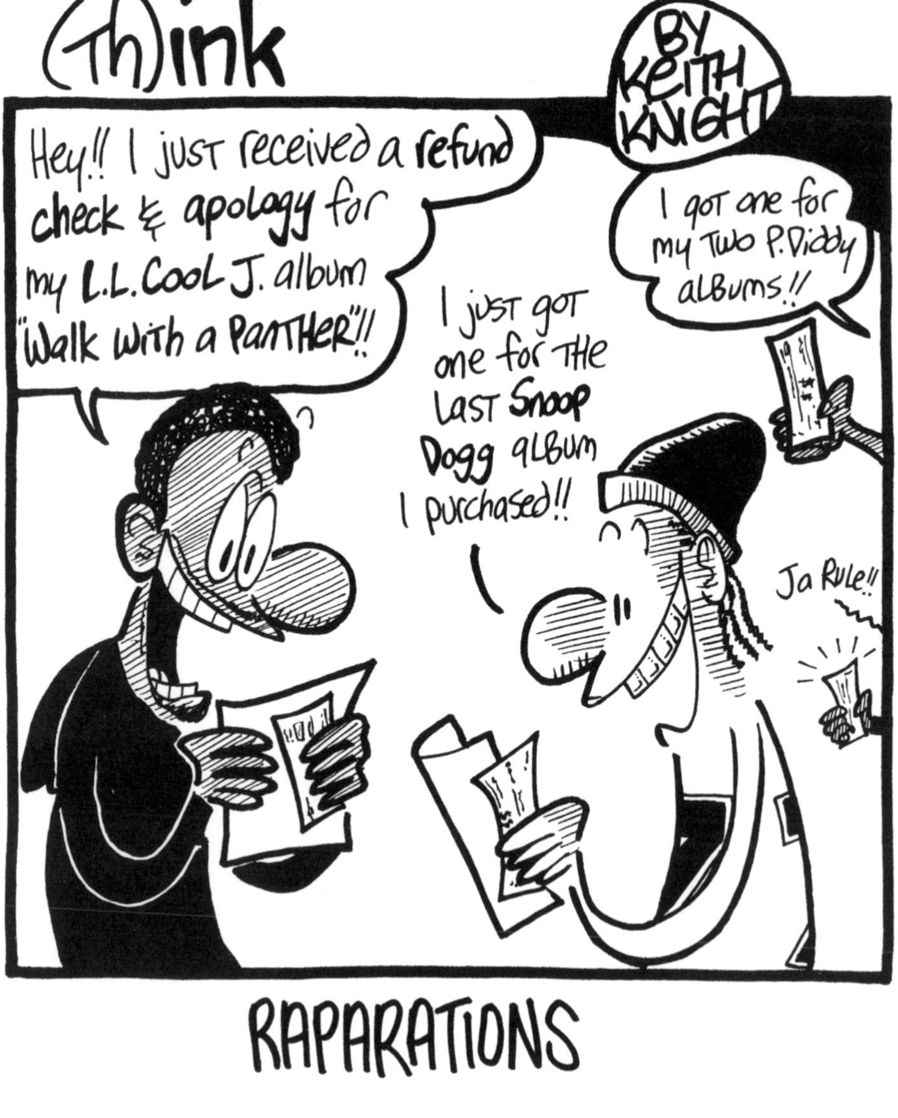
(Th)ink
BY KEITH KNIGHT
Hey!! I just received a refund check & apology for my L.L. Cool J. album "Walk with a Panther"!!
I just got one for the last Snoop Dogg album I purchased!!
I got one for my Two P. Diddy albums!!
Ja Rule!!
RAPARATIONS

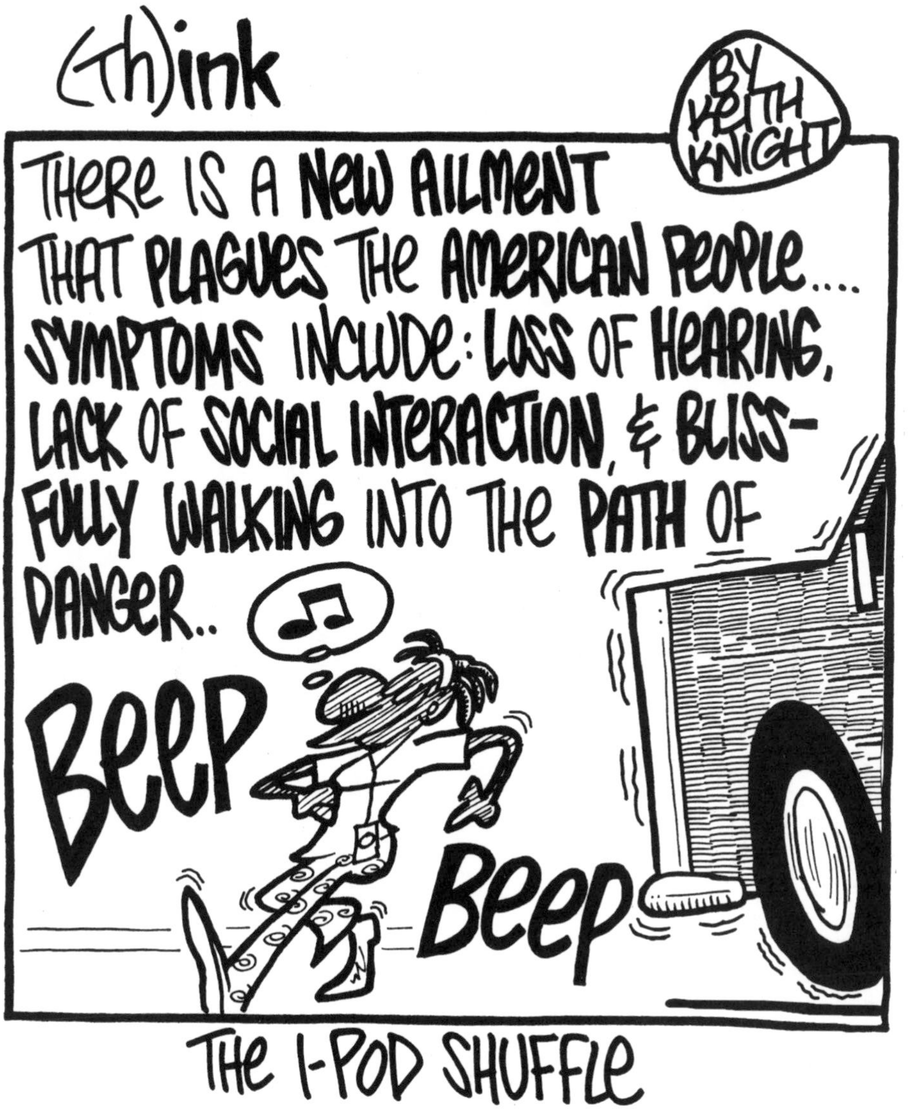
(th)ink
BY KEITH KNIGHT
THERE IS A NEW AILMENT THAT PLAGUES THE AMERICAN PEOPLE.... SYMPTOMS INCLUDE: LOSS OF HEARING, LACK OF SOCIAL INTERACTION, & BLISS-FULLY WALKING INTO THE PATH OF DANGER..
BEEP
BEEP
THE I-POD SHUFFLE

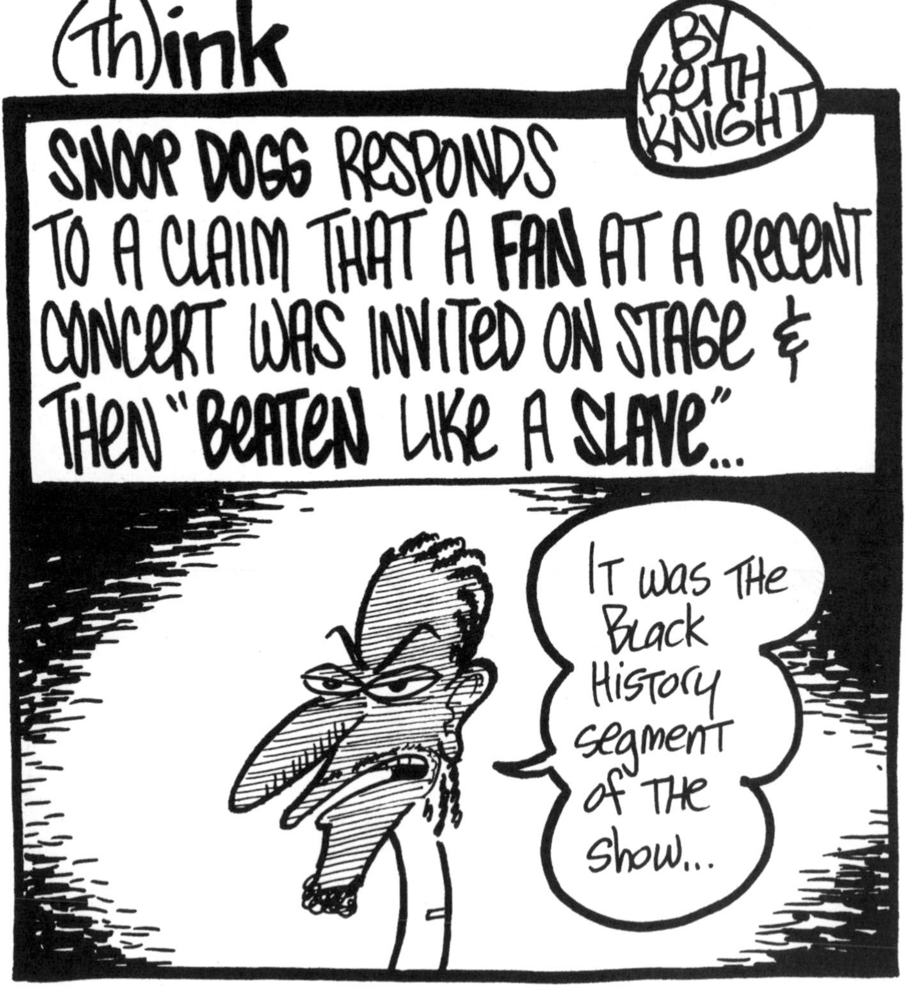
(TH)INK
BY KEITH KNIGHT
SNOOP DOGG RESPONDS TO A CLAIM THAT A FAN AT A RECENT CONCERT WAS INVITED ON STAGE & THEN "BEATEN LIKE A SLAVE"...
IT WAS THE BLACK HISTORY SEGMENT OF THE SHOW...

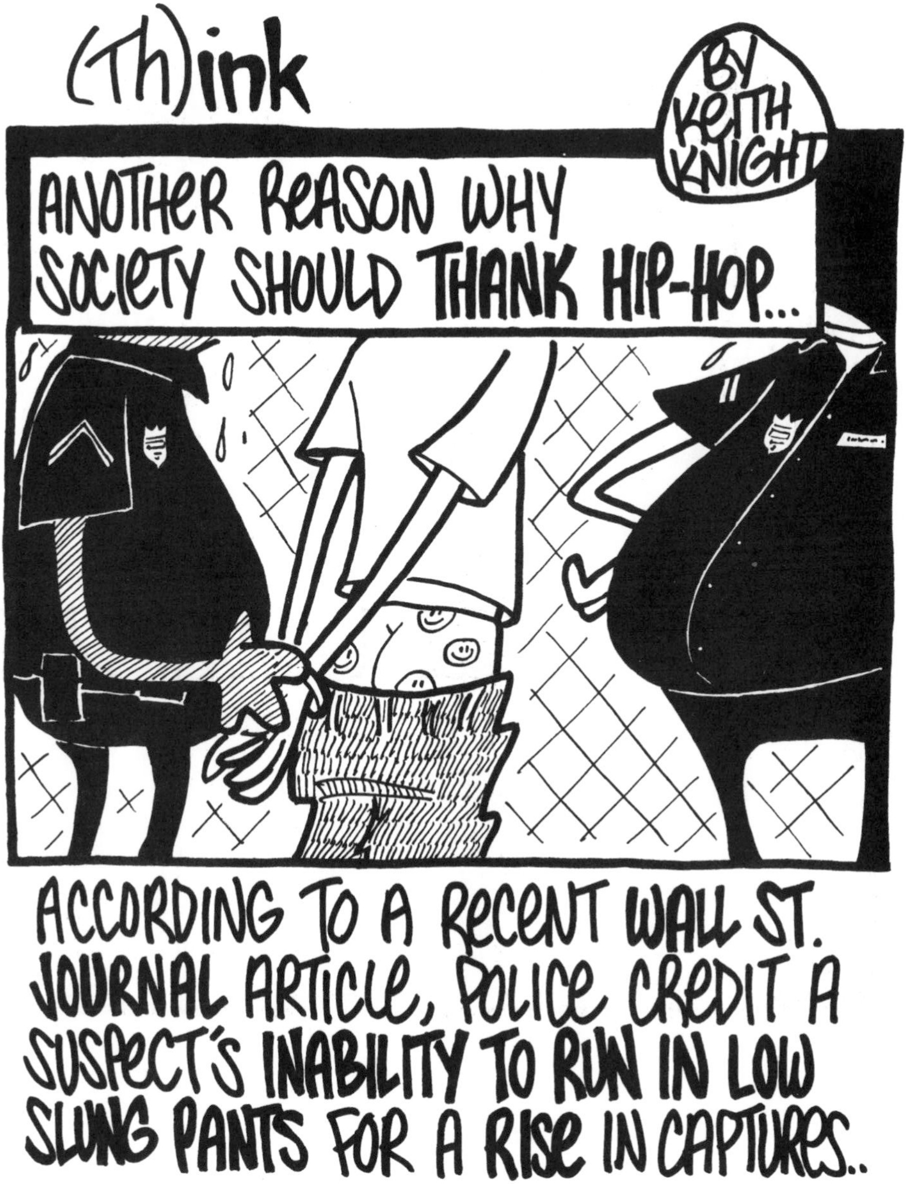
(Th)ink
BY KEITH KNIGHT
ANOTHER REASON WHY SOCIETY SHOULD THANK HIP-HOP...
ACCORDING TO A RECENT WALL ST. JOURNAL ARTICLE, POLICE CREDIT A SUSPECT'S INABILITY TO RUN IN LOW SLUNG PANTS FOR A RISE IN CAPTURES..

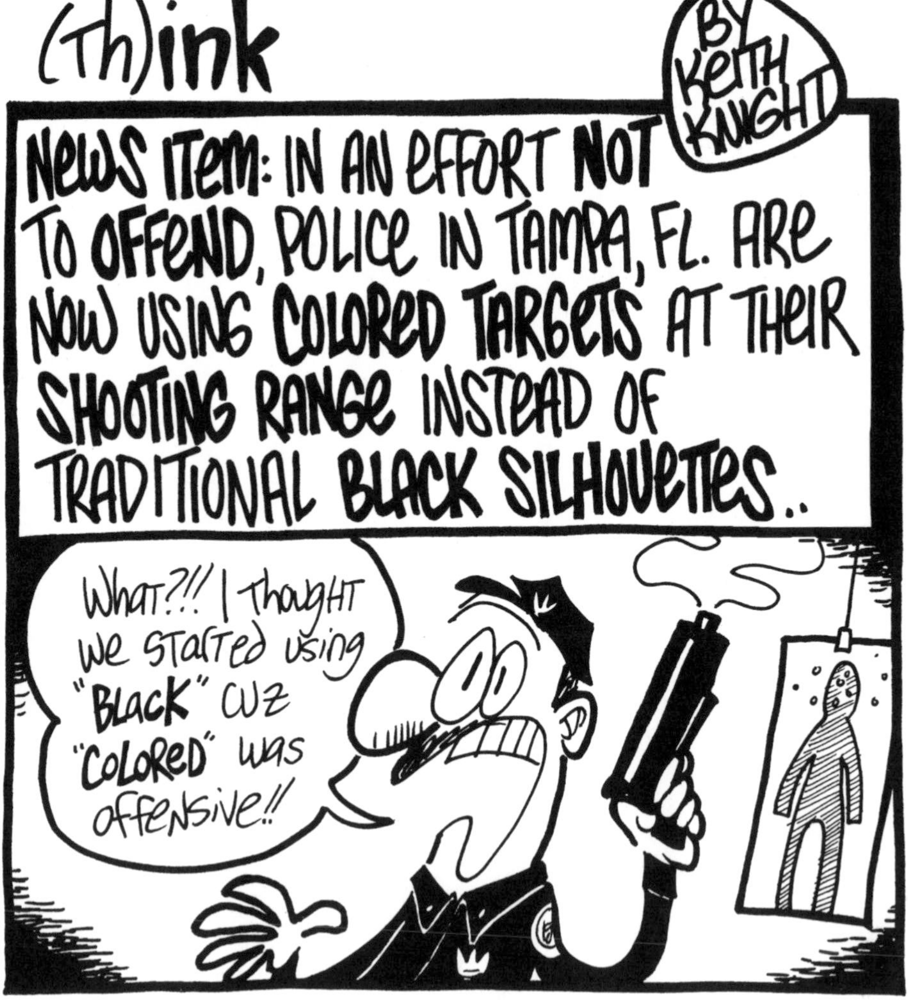
(Th)ink
BY KEITH KNIGHT
NEWS ITEM: IN AN EFFORT NOT TO OFFEND, POLICE IN TAMPA, FL. ARE NOW USING COLORED TARGETS AT THEIR SHOOTING RANGE INSTEAD OF TRADITIONAL BLACK SILHOUETTES..
WHAT?!! I THOUGHT WE STARTED USING "BLACK" CUZ "COLORED" WAS OFFENSIVE!!

(th)ink
BY KEITH KNIGHT
THEN
Don't shoot til you see the whites of their eyes!!
NOW
Don't shoot til you see the Black of their faces!!

(Th)ink
BY KEITH KNIGHT
NEWS ITEM: NEW ORLEANS POLICE OFFICERS ARE FACING BATTERY CHARGES AFTER BEING CAUGHT ON TAPE BEATING A 64 YEAR-OLD MAN ACCUSED OF PUBLIC INTOXICATION...
Man, it feels good to get back to our normal duties!!

(Th)ink
By Keith Knight
News item: The Greensboro N.C. Police Department is being investigated on charges of racial profiling their own black police officers!!
We just wanted to let people know...
...That we treat our rank & file no differently than the average citizen!!
Recently resigned police chief

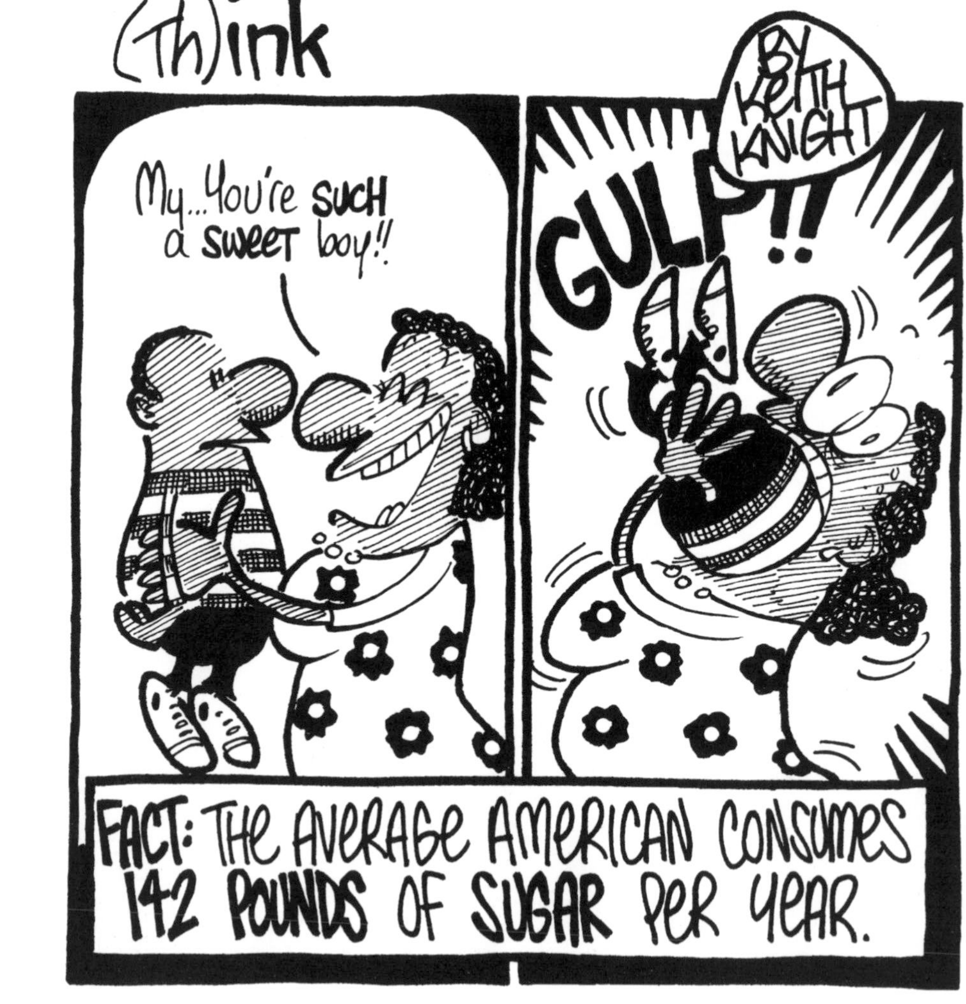

(Th)ink
BY KEITH KNIGHT
My... You're SUCH a SWEET boy!!
GULP!!
FACT: THE AVERAGE AMERICAN CONSUMES 142 POUNDS OF SUGAR PER YEAR.

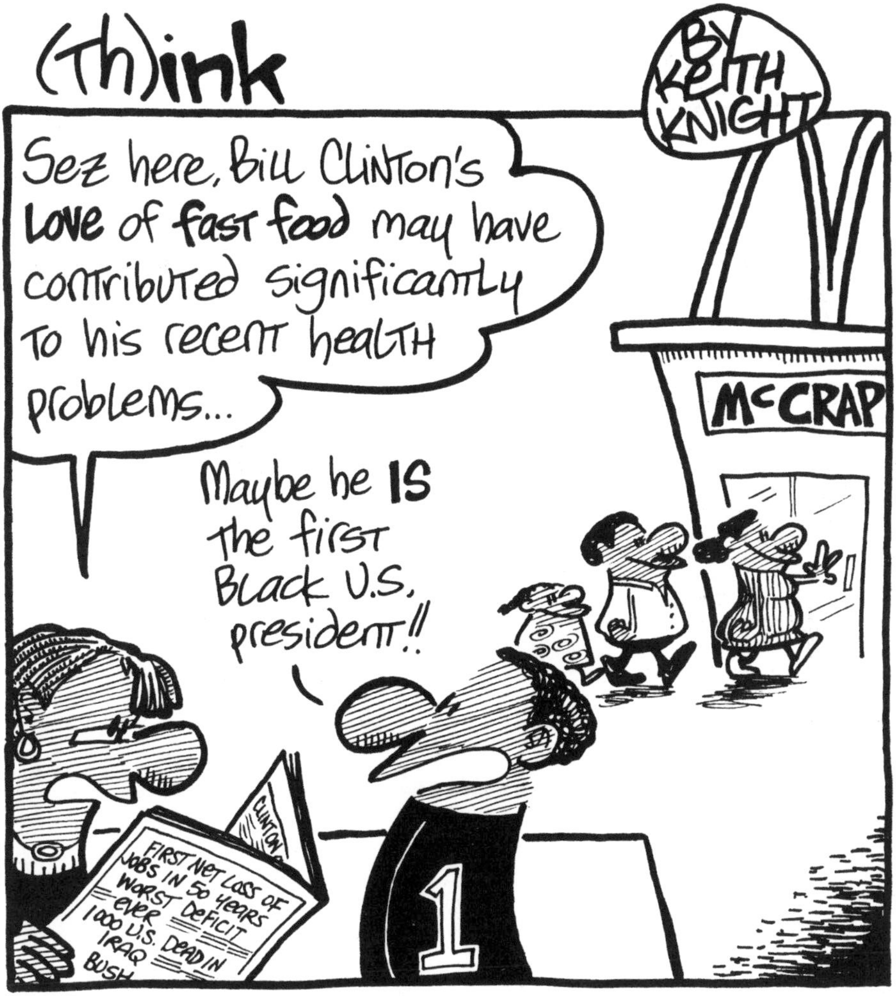
(Th)ink
BY KEITH KNIGHT
Sez here, Bill Clinton's **love** of **fast food** may have contributed significantly to his recent health problems...
Maybe he **IS** the first Black U.S. president!!
McCRAP
CLINTON
FIRST NET LOSS OF JOBS IN 50 YEARS
WORST DEFICIT EVER
1000 U.S. DEAD IN IRAQ
BUSH

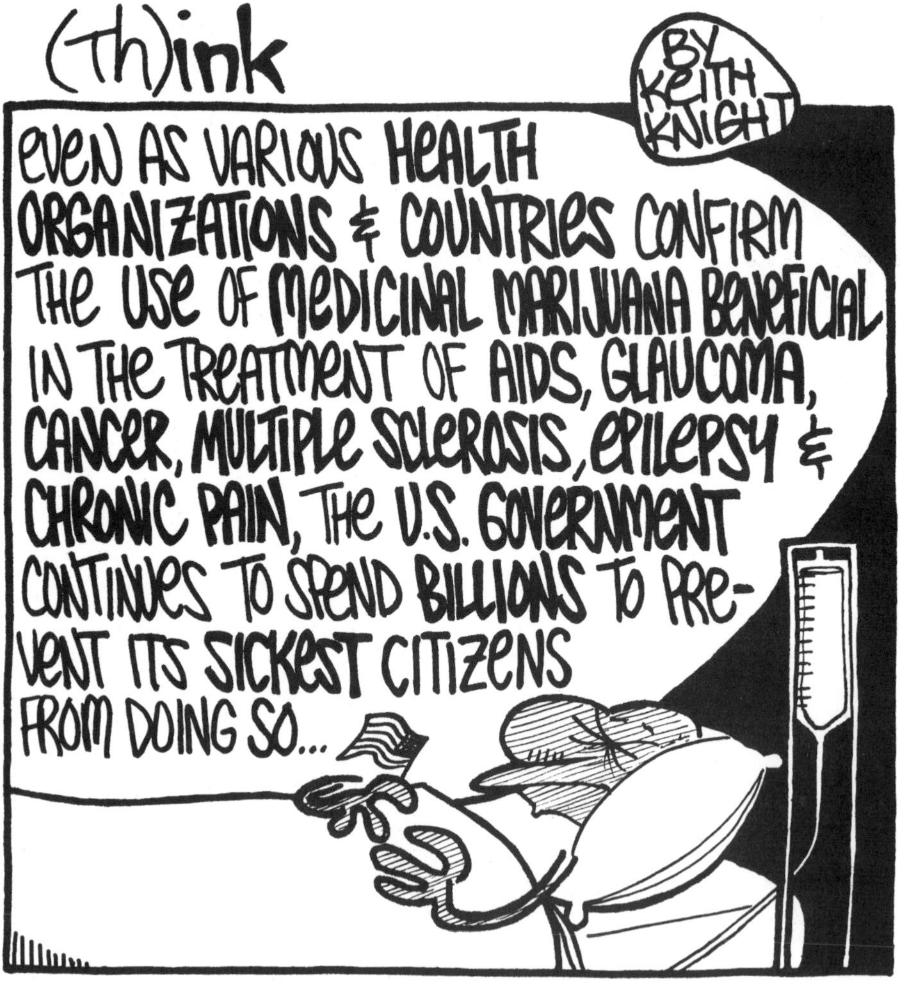
(TH)INK
BY KEITH KNIGHT
EVEN AS VARIOUS HEALTH ORGANIZATIONS & COUNTRIES CONFIRM THE USE OF MEDICINAL MARIJUANA BENEFICIAL IN THE TREATMENT OF AIDS, GLAUCOMA, CANCER, MULTIPLE SCLEROSIS, EPILEPSY & CHRONIC PAIN, THE U.S. GOVERNMENT CONTINUES TO SPEND BILLIONS TO PRE-VENT ITS SICKEST CITIZENS FROM DOING SO...

WAITING TO INHALE

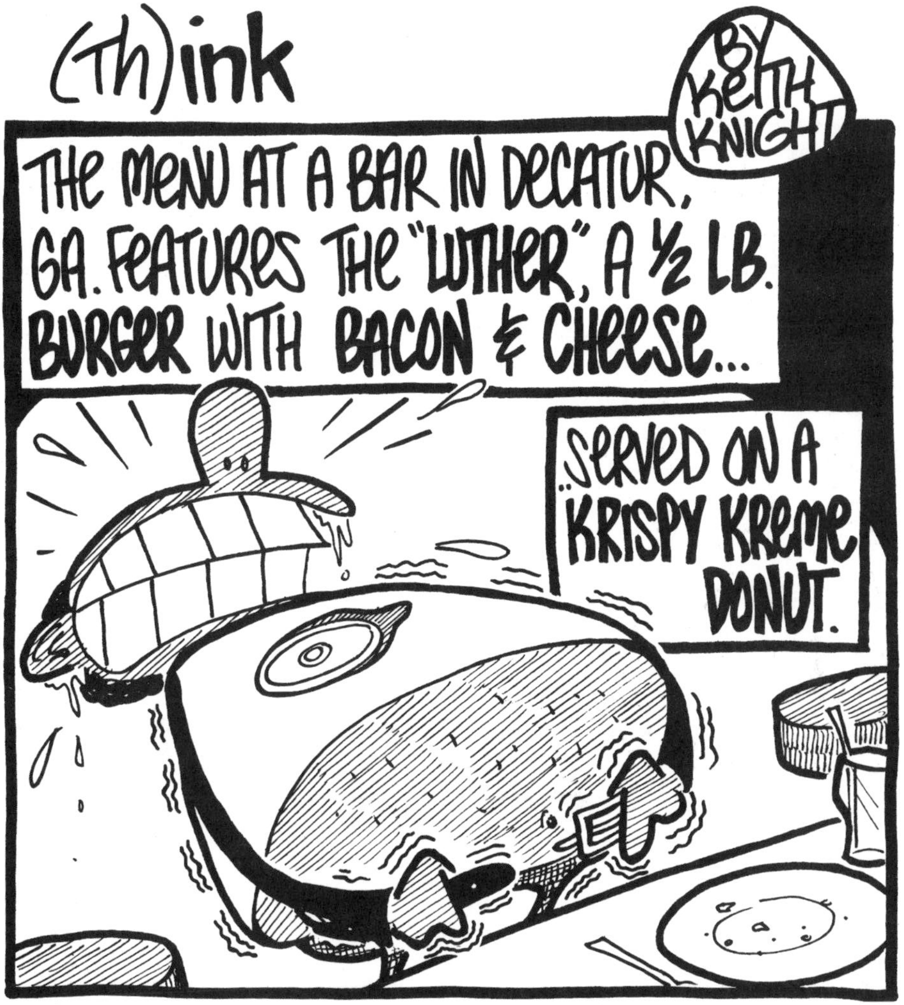
(Th)ink
By Keith Knight
The menu at a bar in Decatur, GA. features the "Luther", a ½ lb. burger with bacon & cheese...
...served on a Krispy Kreme donut.

The Bible Belt No Longer Fits

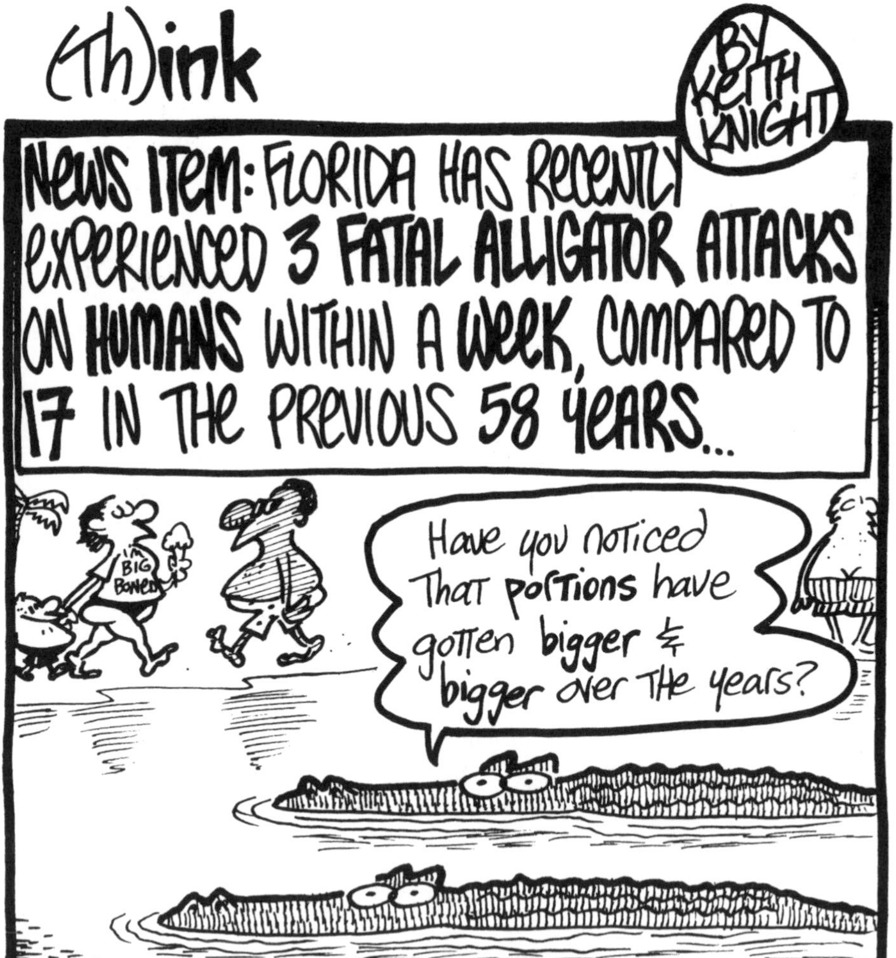
(Th)ink
BY KEITH KNIGHT
NEWS ITEM: FLORIDA HAS RECENTLY EXPERIENCED 3 FATAL ALLIGATOR ATTACKS ON HUMANS WITHIN A WEEK, COMPARED TO 17 IN THE PREVIOUS 58 YEARS...
I'M BIG BONED
Have you noticed That portions have gotten bigger & bigger over The years?

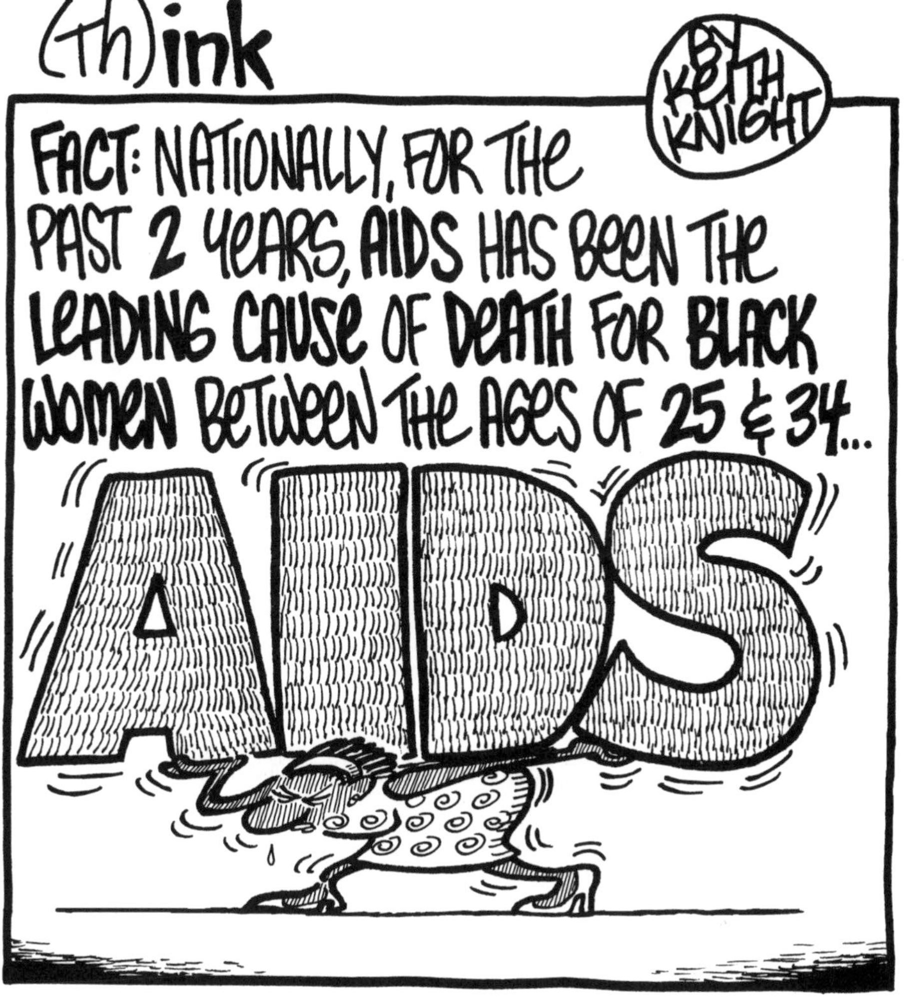
(th)ink
BY KEITH KNIGHT
FACT: NATIONALLY, FOR THE PAST 2 YEARS, AIDS HAS BEEN THE LEADING CAUSE OF DEATH FOR BLACK WOMEN BETWEEN THE AGES OF 25 & 34...
AIDS

BLACK WOMAN'S BURDEN

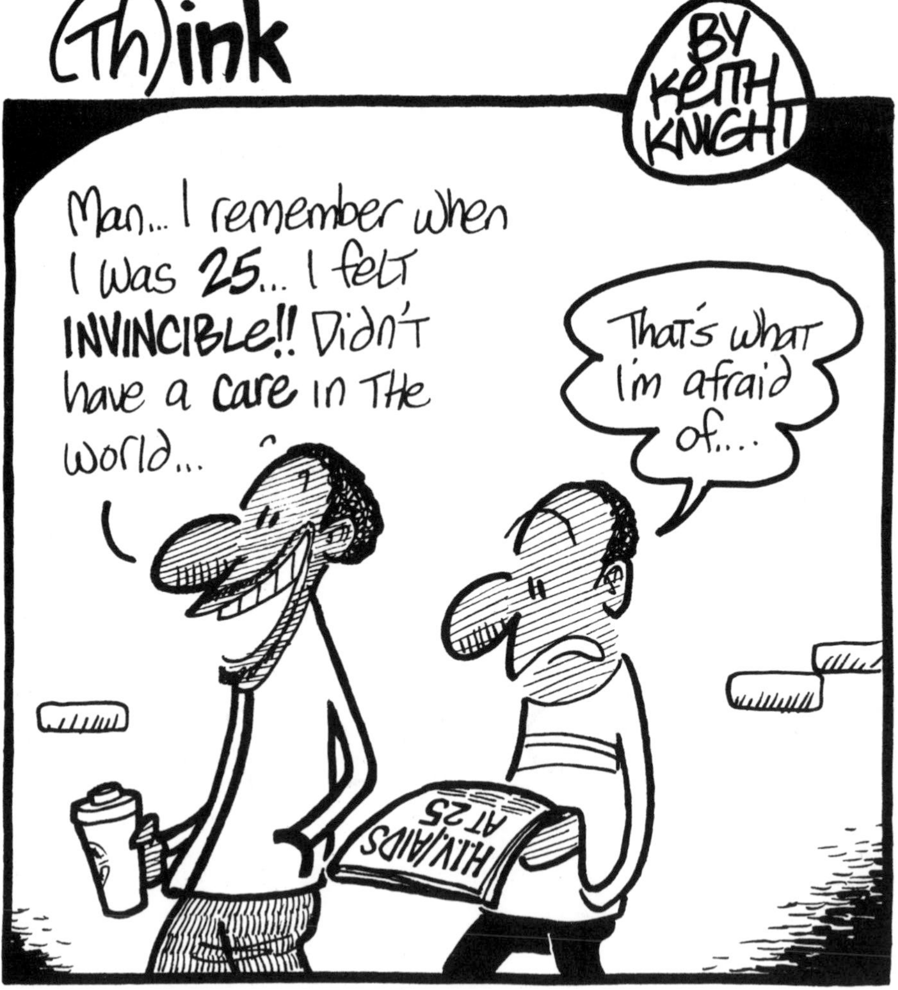
(Th)ink
BY KEITH KNIGHT
Man... I remember when I was 25... I felt INVINCIBLE!! Didn't have a care in the world...
That's what I'm afraid of....
HIV/AIDS AT 25

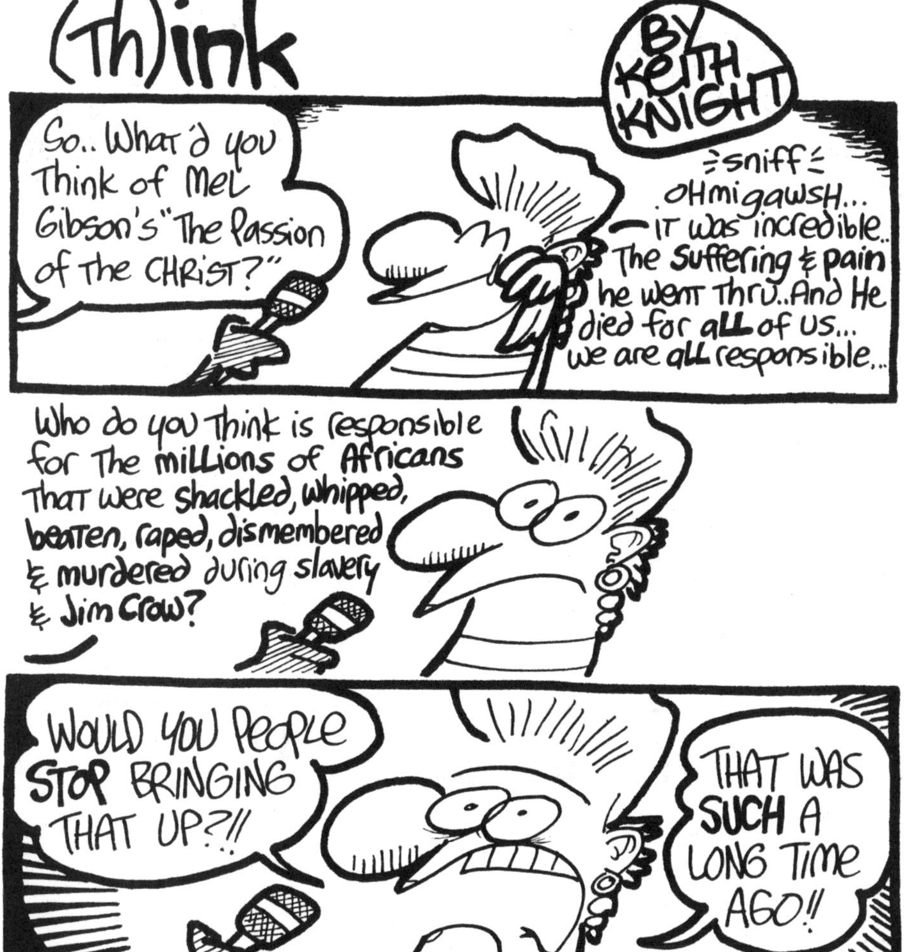
(Th)ink
BY KEITH KNIGHT
So.. What'd you Think of Mel Gibson's "The Passion of the CHRIST?"
sniff
OHmigawsH... it was incredible.. The suffering & pain he went thru..And He died for all of us... we are all responsible...
Who do you Think is responsible for The millions of Africans That were shackled, whipped, beaten, raped, dismembered & murdered during slavery & Jim Crow?
WOULD YOU PEOPLE STOP BRINGING THAT UP?!!
THAT WAS SUCH A LONG TIME AGO!!

(th)ink

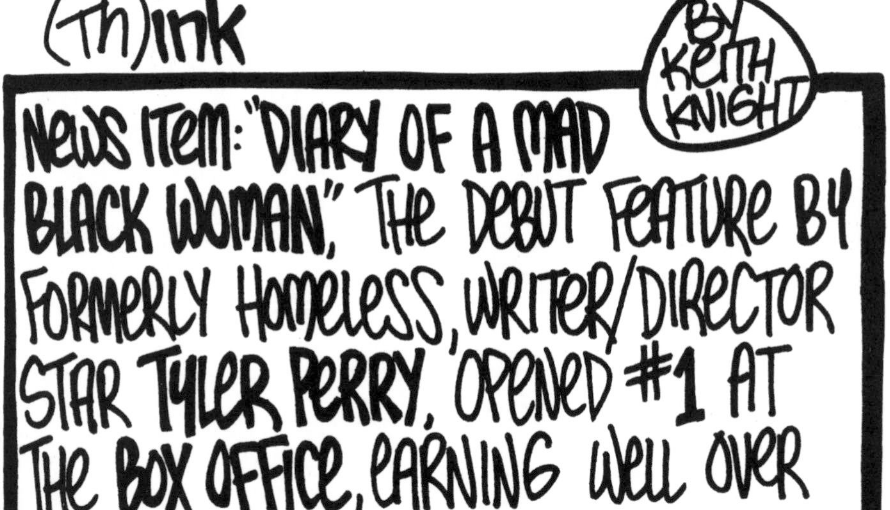
By Keith Knight
News Item: "Diary of a Mad Black Woman," the debut feature by formerly homeless, writer/director star Tyler Perry, opened #1 at the box office, earning well over four times what it cost to make...

DIARY OF A HAPPY BLACK MAN

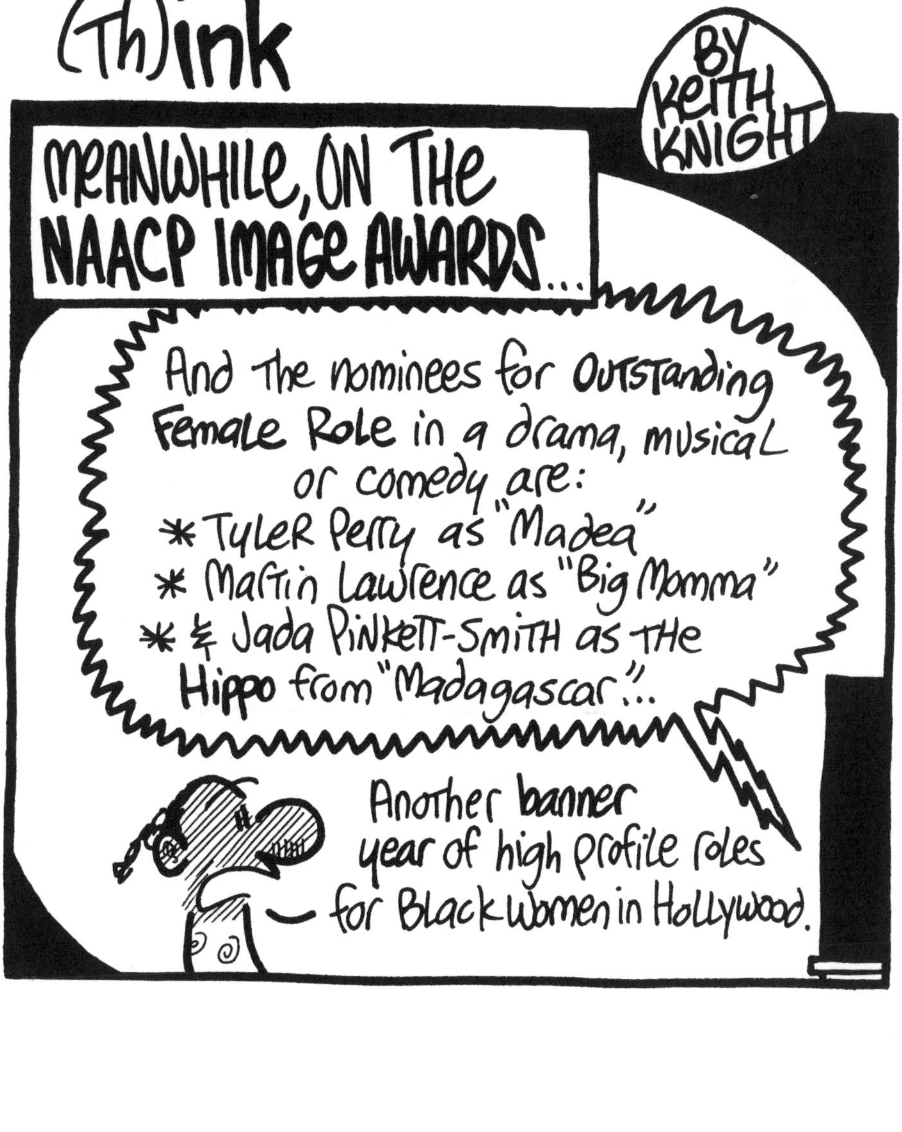
(Th)ink
BY KEITH KNIGHT
MEANWHILE, ON THE NAACP IMAGE AWARDS...
And the nominees for OUTSTANDING Female Role in a drama, musical or comedy are:
* Tyler Perry as "Madea"
* Martin Lawrence as "Big Momma"
* & Jada Pinkett-Smith as the Hippo from "Madagascar"...
Another banner year of high profile roles for Black Women in Hollywood.

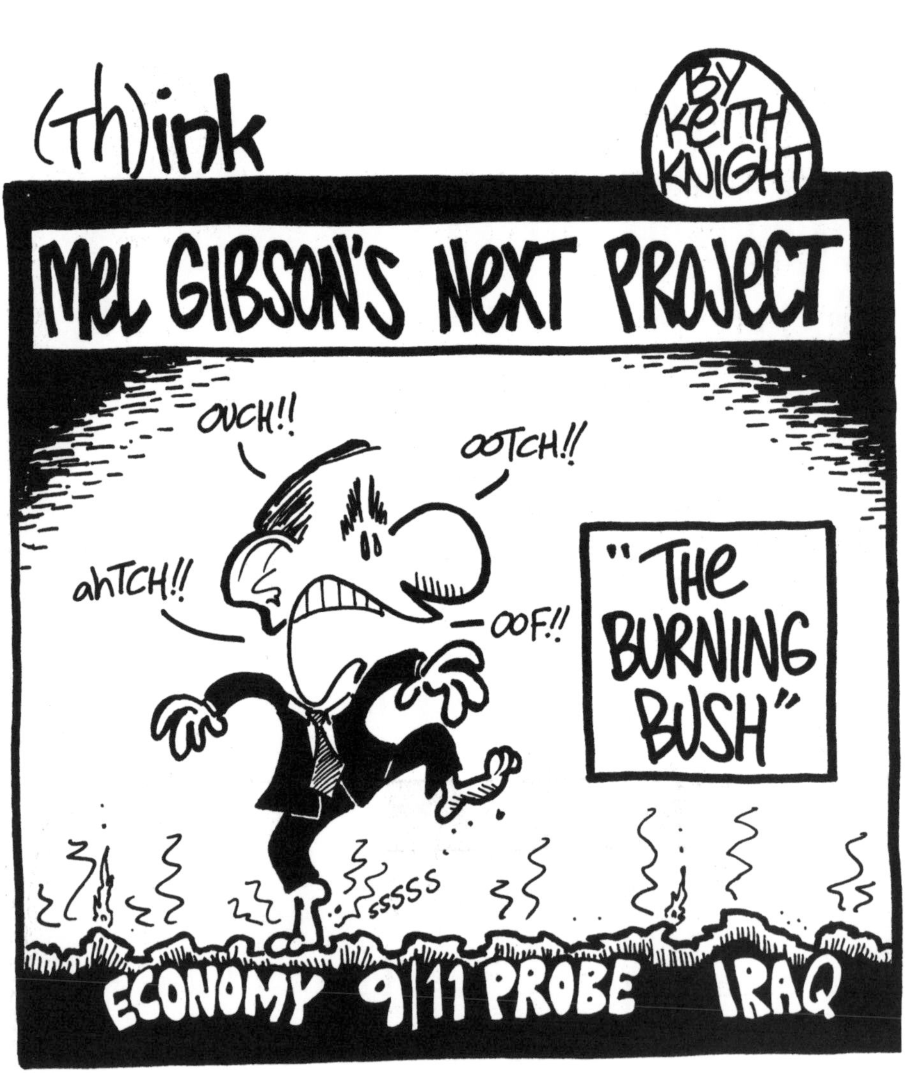
(TH)ink
BY KEITH KNIGHT
MEL GIBSON'S NEXT PROJECT
OUCH!!
OOTCH!!
ahTCH!!
OOF!!
SSSSS
"THE BURNING BUSH"
ECONOMY
9/11 PROBE
IRAQ

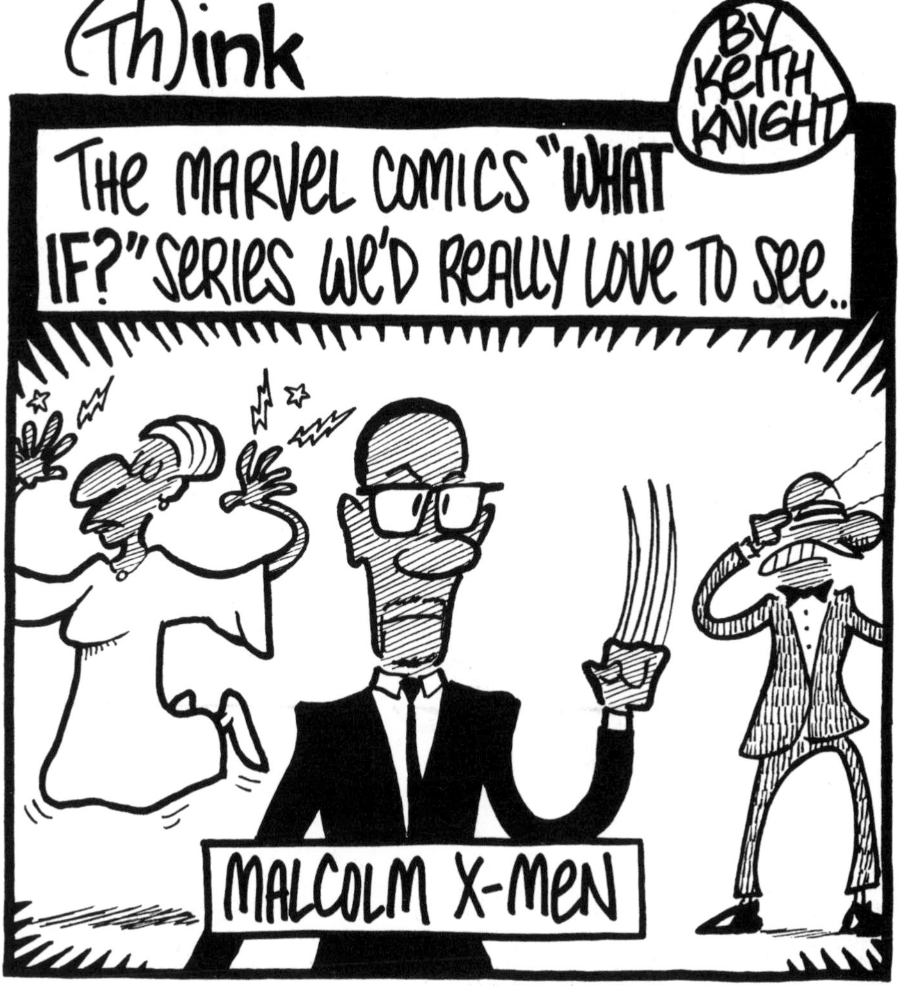
(Th)ink
BY KEITH KNIGHT
THE MARVEL COMICS "WHAT IF?" SERIES WE'D REALLY LOVE TO SEE..
MALCOLM X-MEN

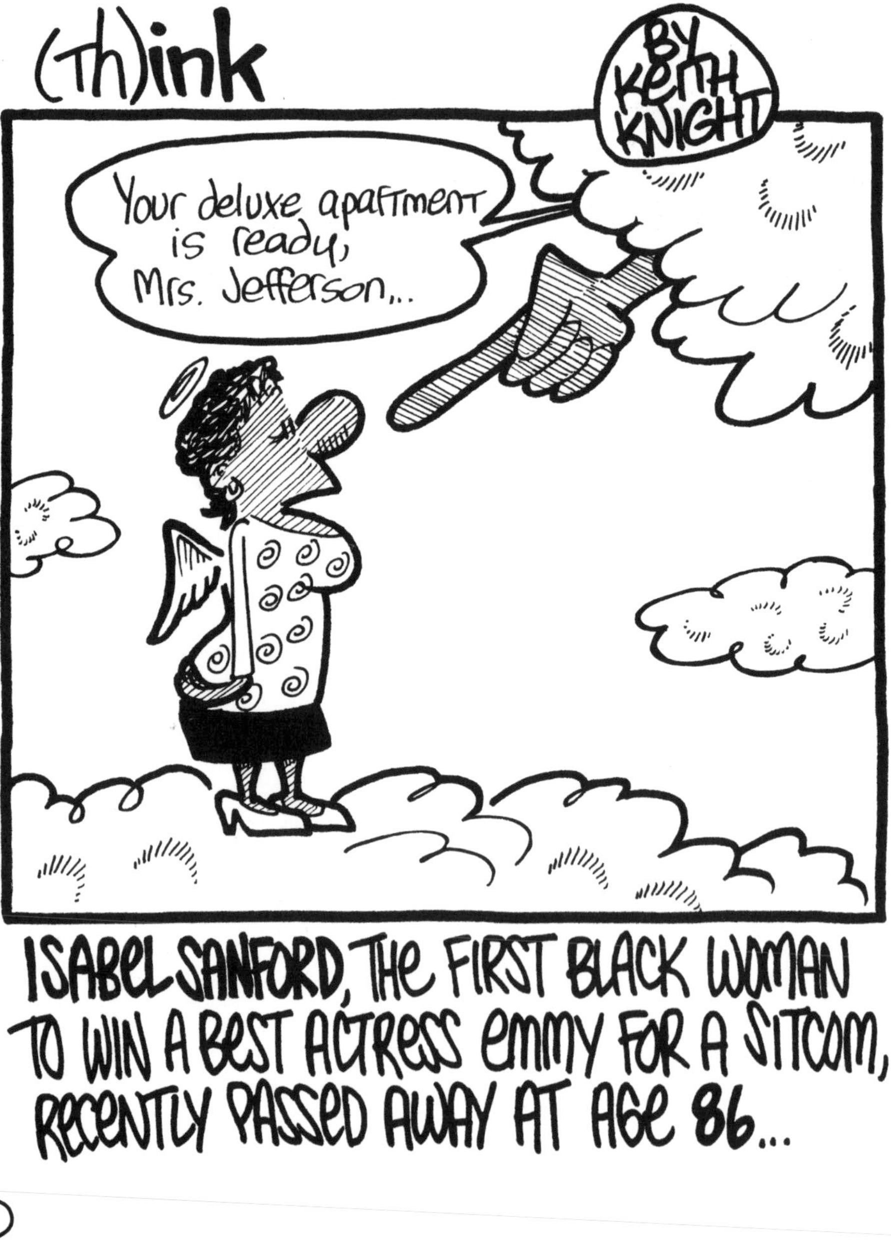
(th)ink
BY KEITH KNIGHT
Your deluxe apartment is ready, Mrs. Jefferson...
ISABEL SANFORD, THE FIRST BLACK WOMAN TO WIN A BEST ACTRESS EMMY FOR A SITCOM, RECENTLY PASSED AWAY AT AGE 86...

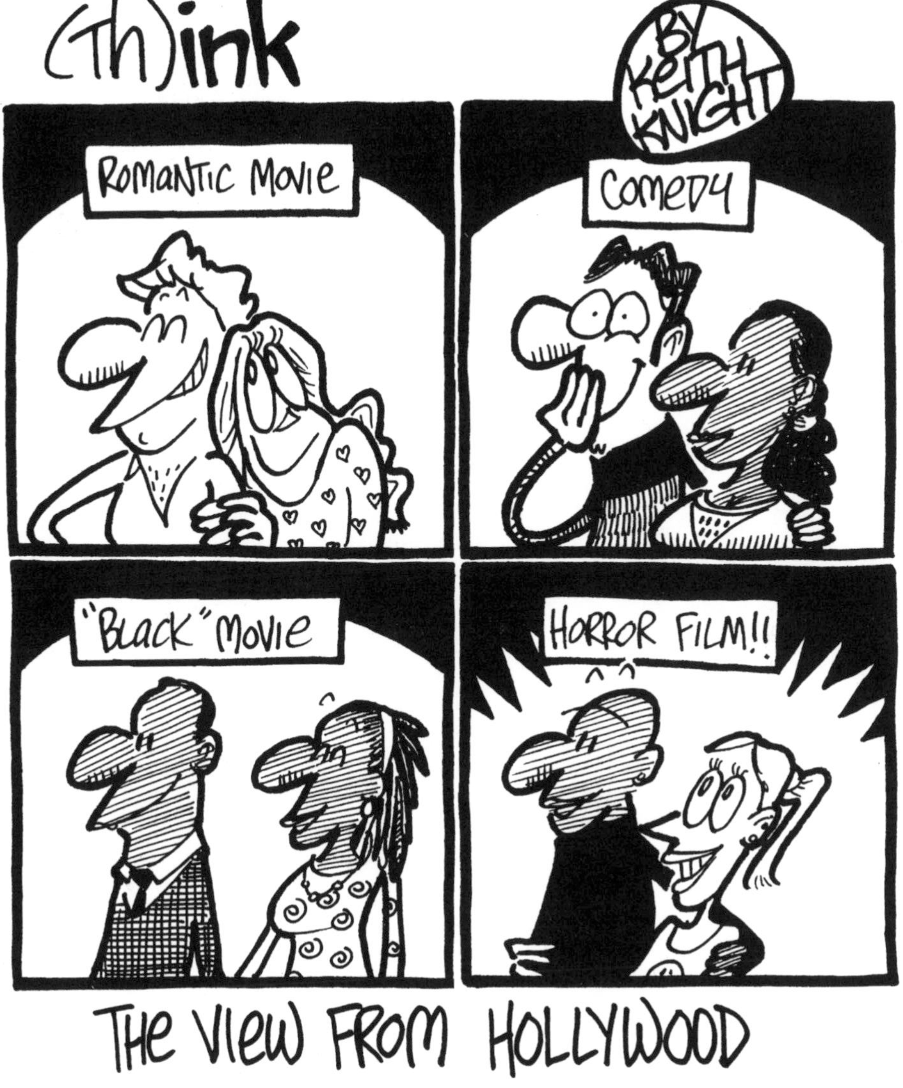

(TH)INK
BY KEITH KNIGHT
ROMANTIC MOVIE
COMEDY
"BLACK" MOVIE
HORROR FILM!!
THE VIEW FROM HOLLYWOOD

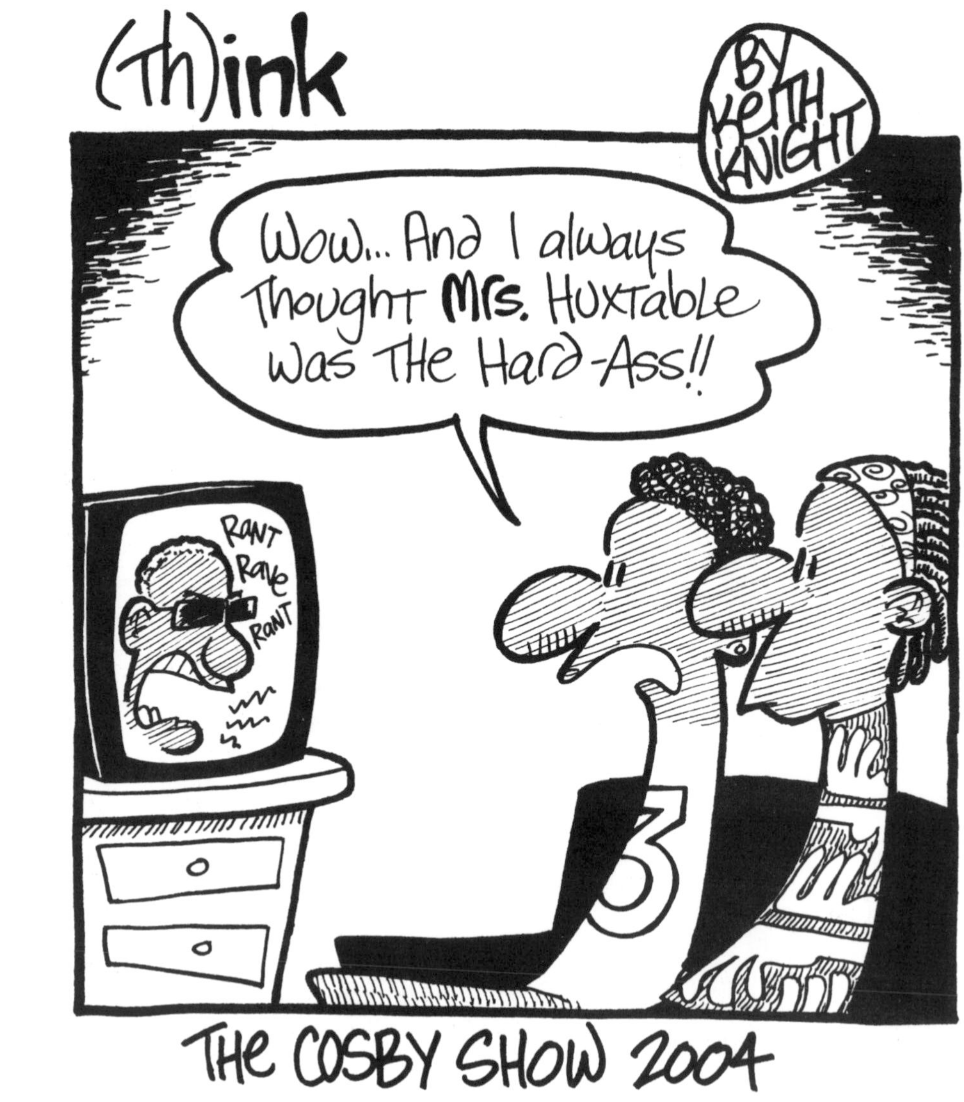
(Th)ink
By Keith Knight
Wow... And I always Thought Mrs. Huxtable was The Hard-Ass!!
RanT Rave RanT
3

THE COSBY SHOW 2004

(th)ink

BY KEITH KNIGHT

NEWS ITEM: ACCLAIMED TAP DANCER/ACTOR GREGORY HINES, ONE OF THE MOST VERSATILE PEFORMERS OF OUR TIME, RECENTLY SUCCUMBED TO CANCER AT THE AGE OF 57...

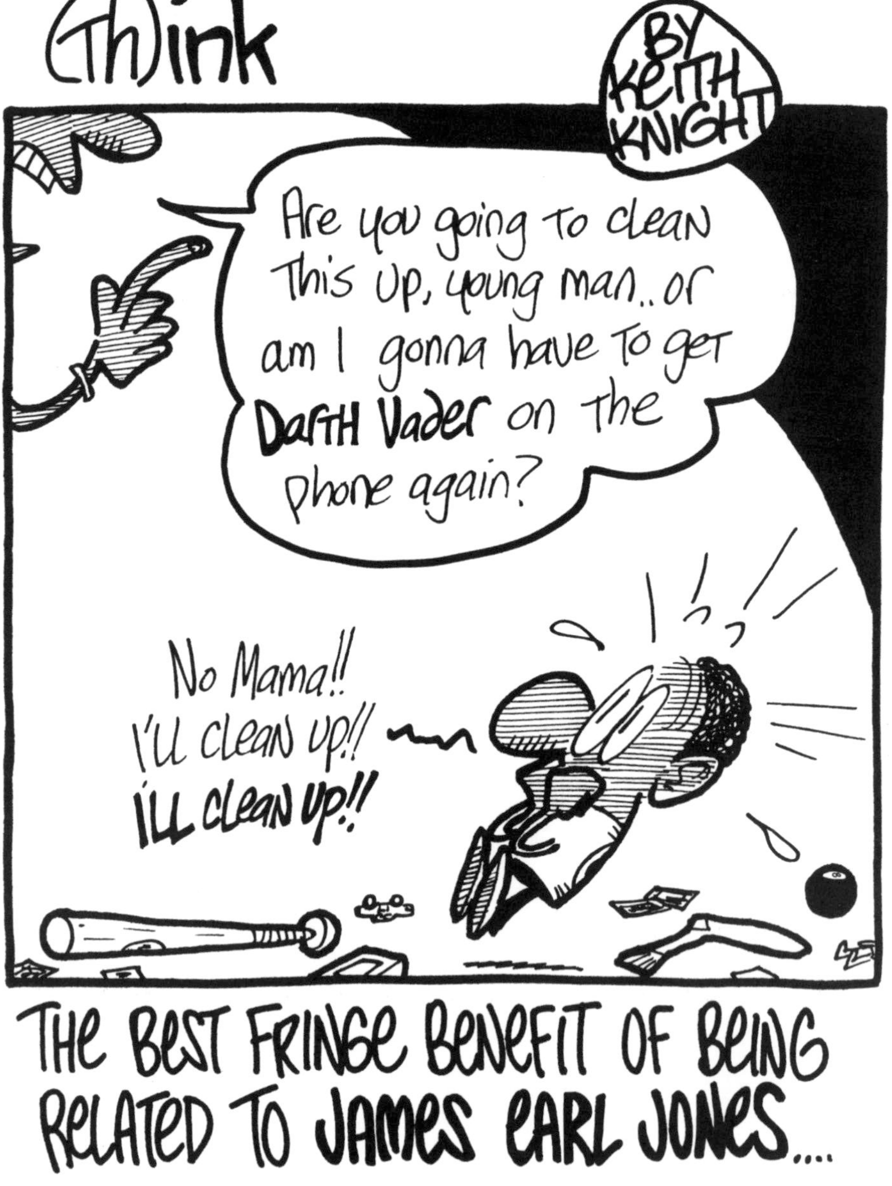
(Th)ink
BY KEITH KNIGHT
Are you going to clean This up, young man.. or am I gonna have to get DARTH Vader on the phone again?
No Mama!! I'll clean up!! I'LL CLEAN UP!!
THE BEST FRINGE BENEFIT OF BEING RELATED TO JAMES EARL JONES....

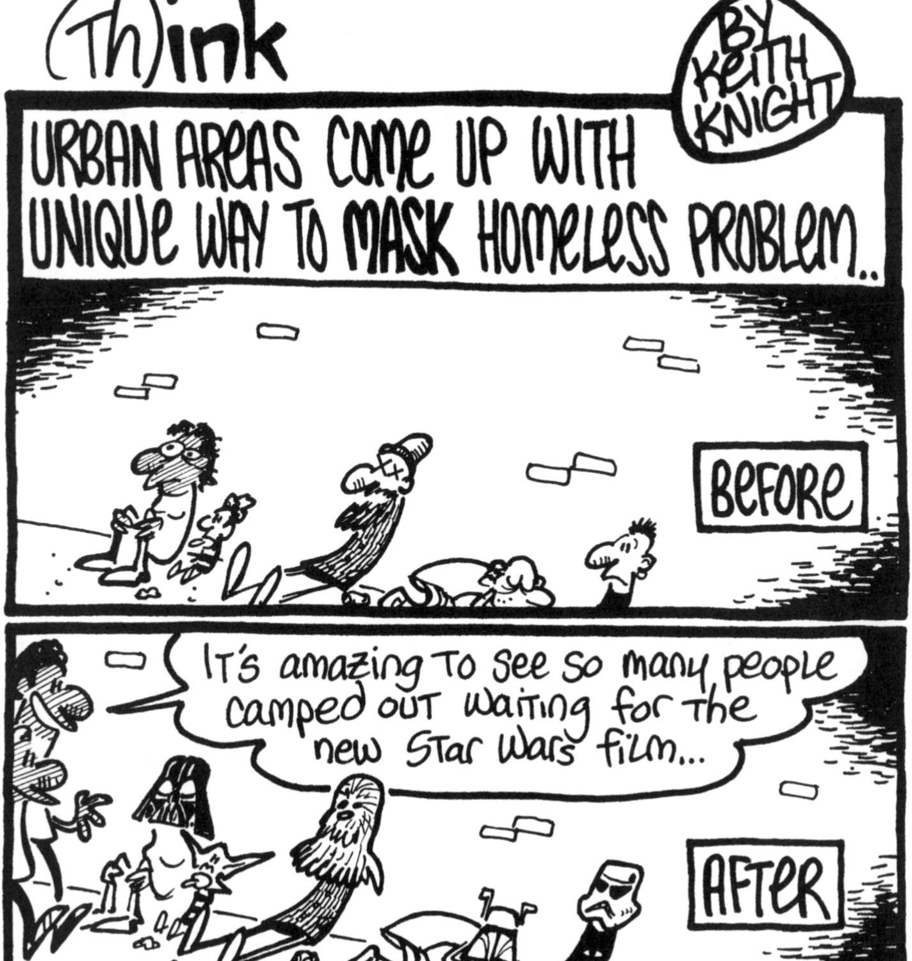
(Th)ink
BY KEITH KNIGHT
URBAN AREAS COME UP WITH UNIQUE WAY TO MASK HOMELESS PROBLEM..
BEFORE
IT'S amazing TO see so many people camped out waiting for the new Star Wars film...
AFTER

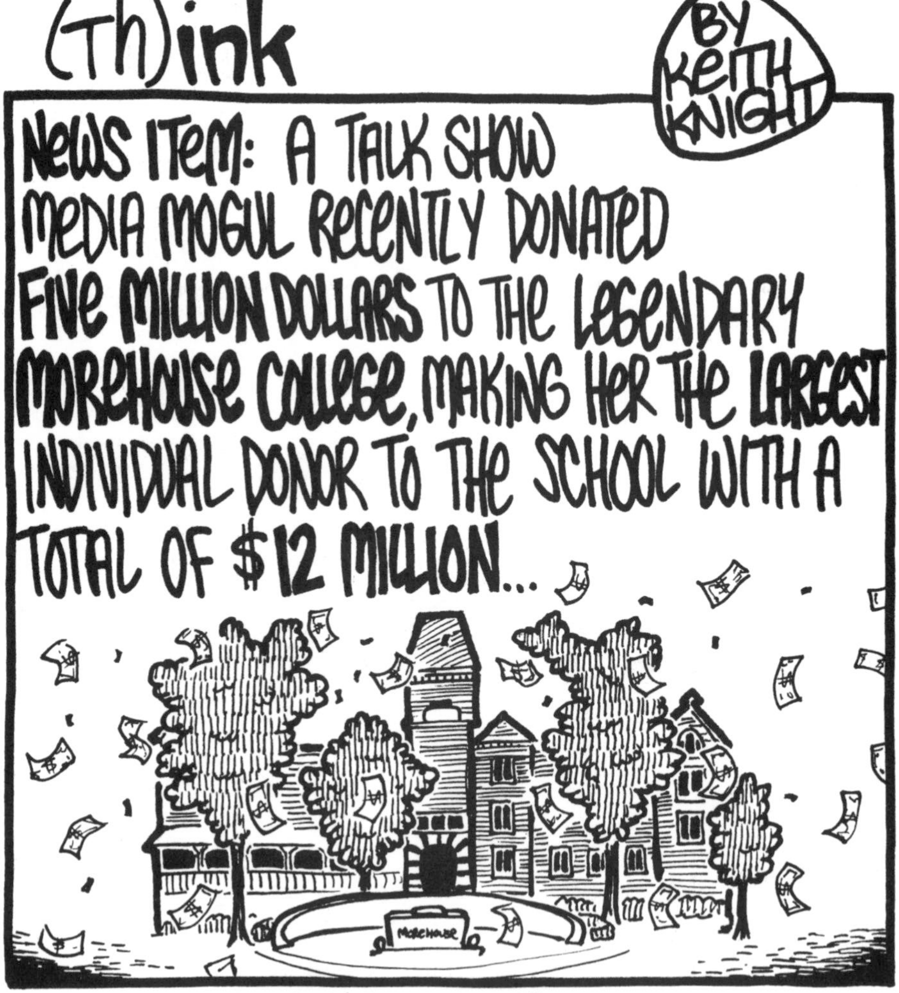
(TH)ink
BY KEITH KNIGHT
NEWS ITEM: A TALK SHOW MEDIA MOGUL RECENTLY DONATED FIVE MILLION DOLLARS TO THE LEGENDARY MOREHOUSE COLLEGE, MAKING HER THE LARGEST INDIVIDUAL DONOR TO THE SCHOOL WITH A TOTAL OF $12 MILLION...
MOREHOUSE

OPRAH WINDFALL

(Th)ink
BY KEITH KNIGHT
PAIN
HUMOR
SATIRE
GENIUS
PROFANITY
VULNERABILITY
ANGER
HUMANITY
WITHOUT HIM, THERE WOULD BE NO EDDIE MURPHY, NO CHRIS ROCK, NO "IN LIVING COLOR", NO "BOONDOCKS", NO DAVE CHAPPELLE,
NO (TH)INK!!
RICHARD PRYOR
1940-2005

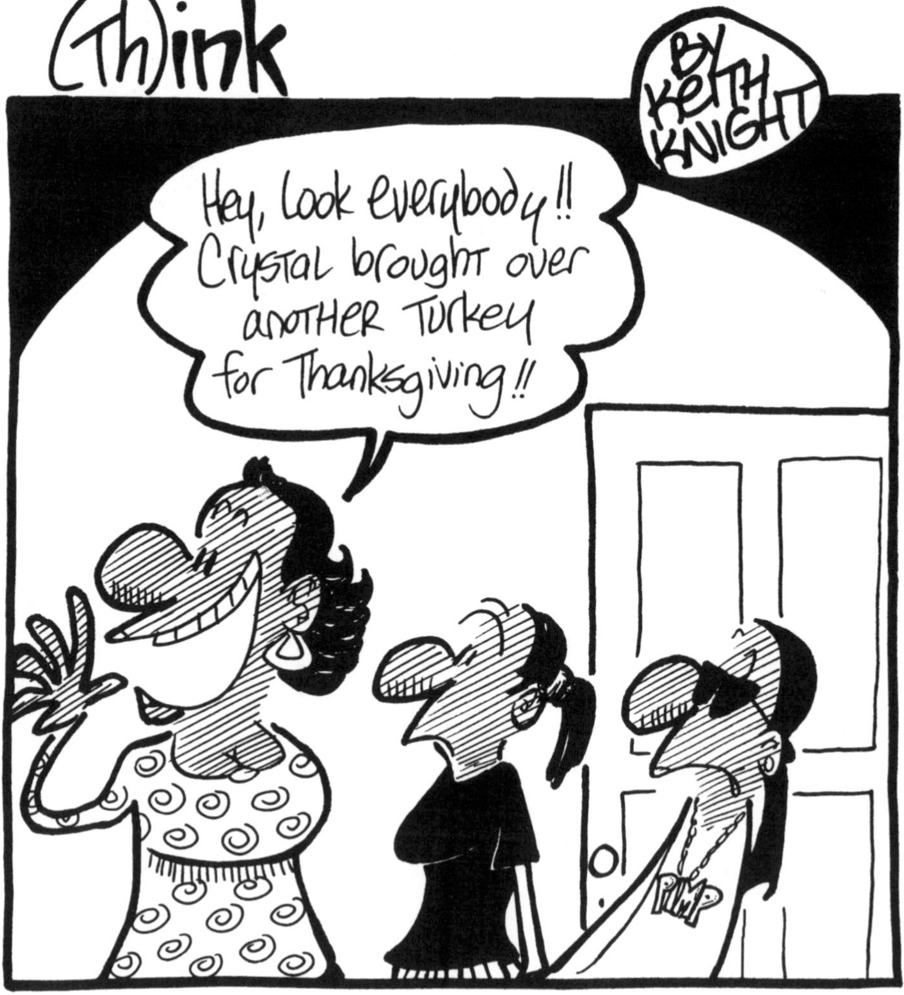

(Th)ink
BY KEITH KNIGHT
Hey, look everybody!! Crystal brought over another Turkey for Thanksgiving!!
PIMP

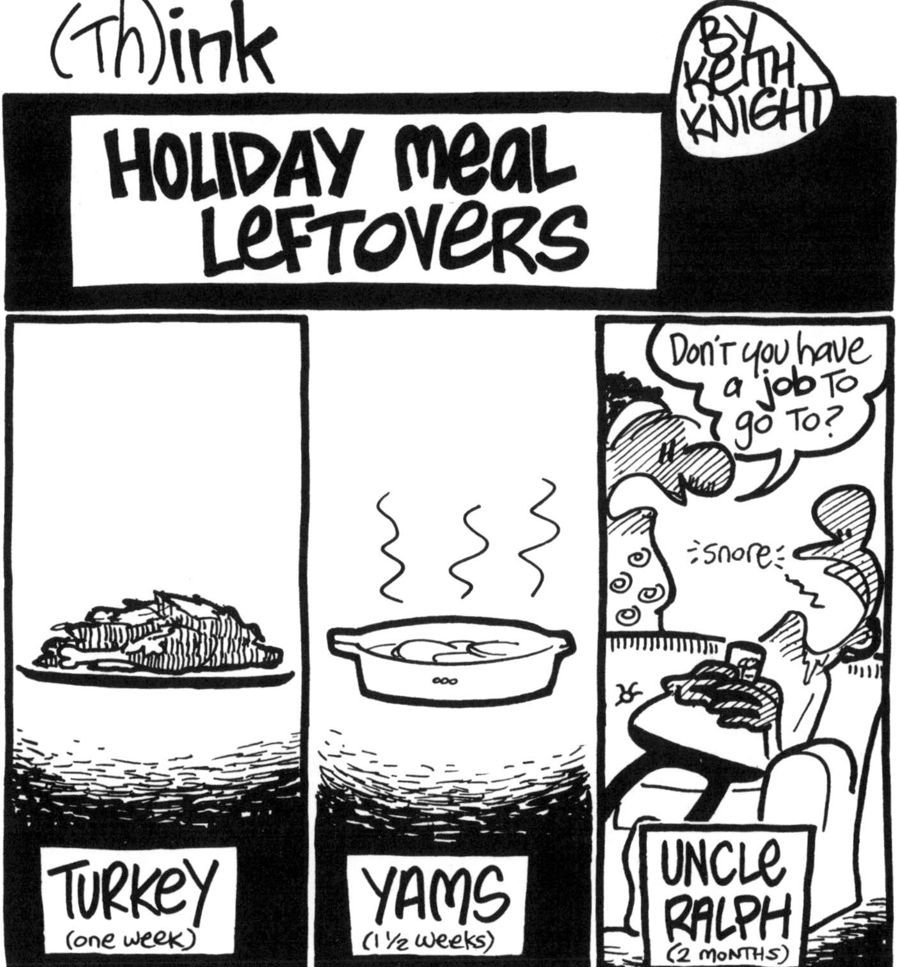
(Th)ink
BY KEITH KNIGHT
HOLIDAY MEAL LEFTOVERS
TURKEY
(one week)
YAMS
(1 ½ weeks)
Don't you have a job to go to?
snore
UNCLE RALPH
(2 MONTHS)

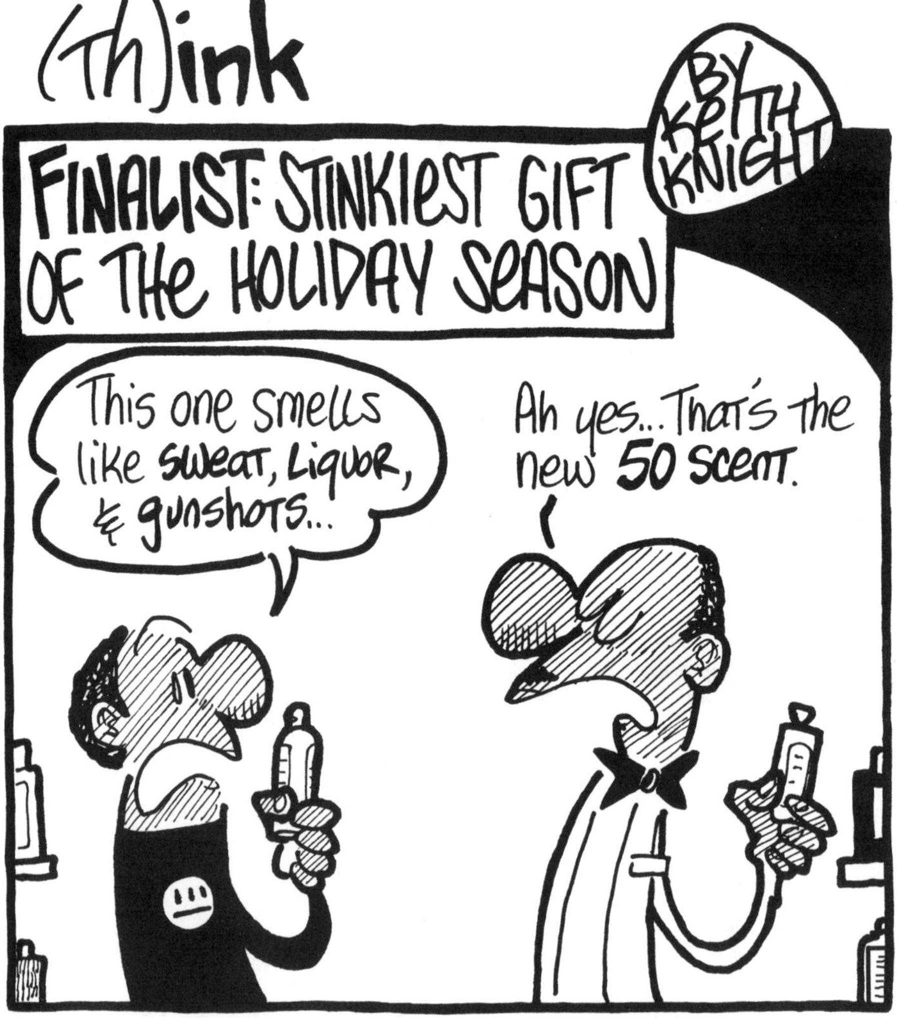
(Th)ink
By Keith Knight
FINALIST: STINKIEST GIFT OF THE HOLIDAY SEASON
This one smells like sweat, liquor, & gunshots...
Ah yes... That's the new 50 scent.
RAPPER-THEMED COLOGNE

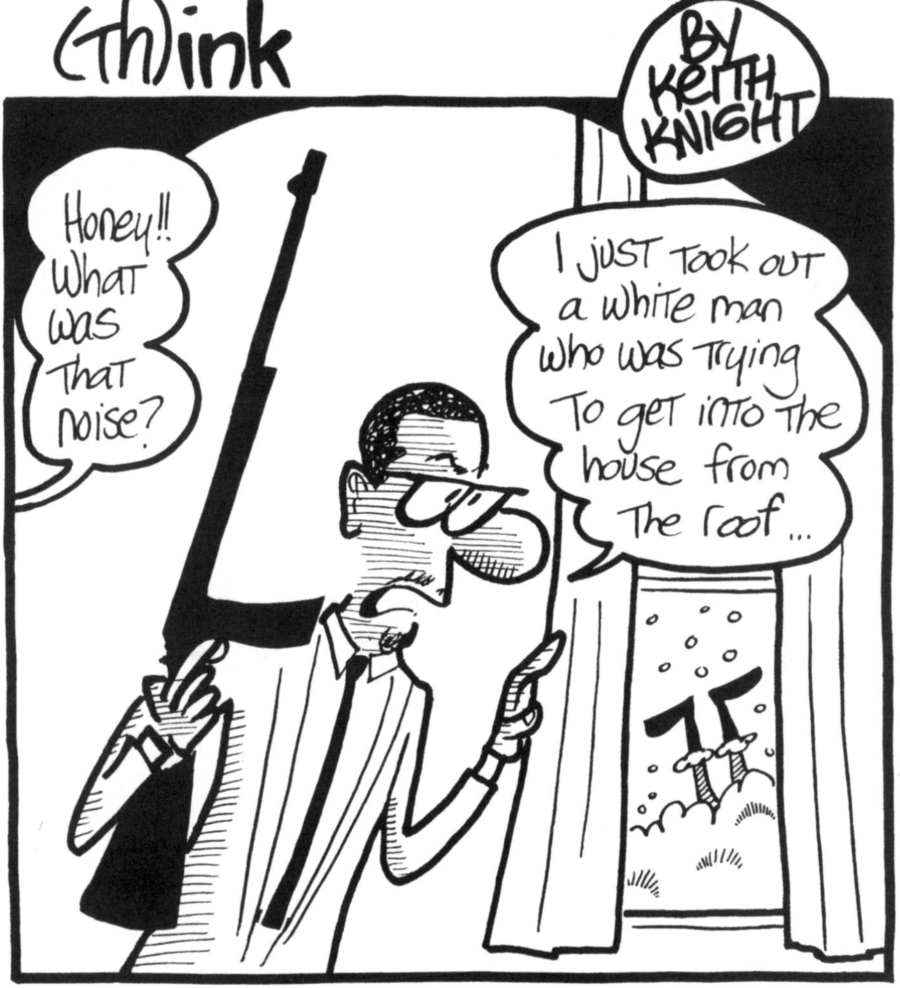
(th)ink
By Keith Knight
Honey!! What was that noise?
I just took out a white man who was trying to get into the house from the roof...

MALCOLM X-MAS

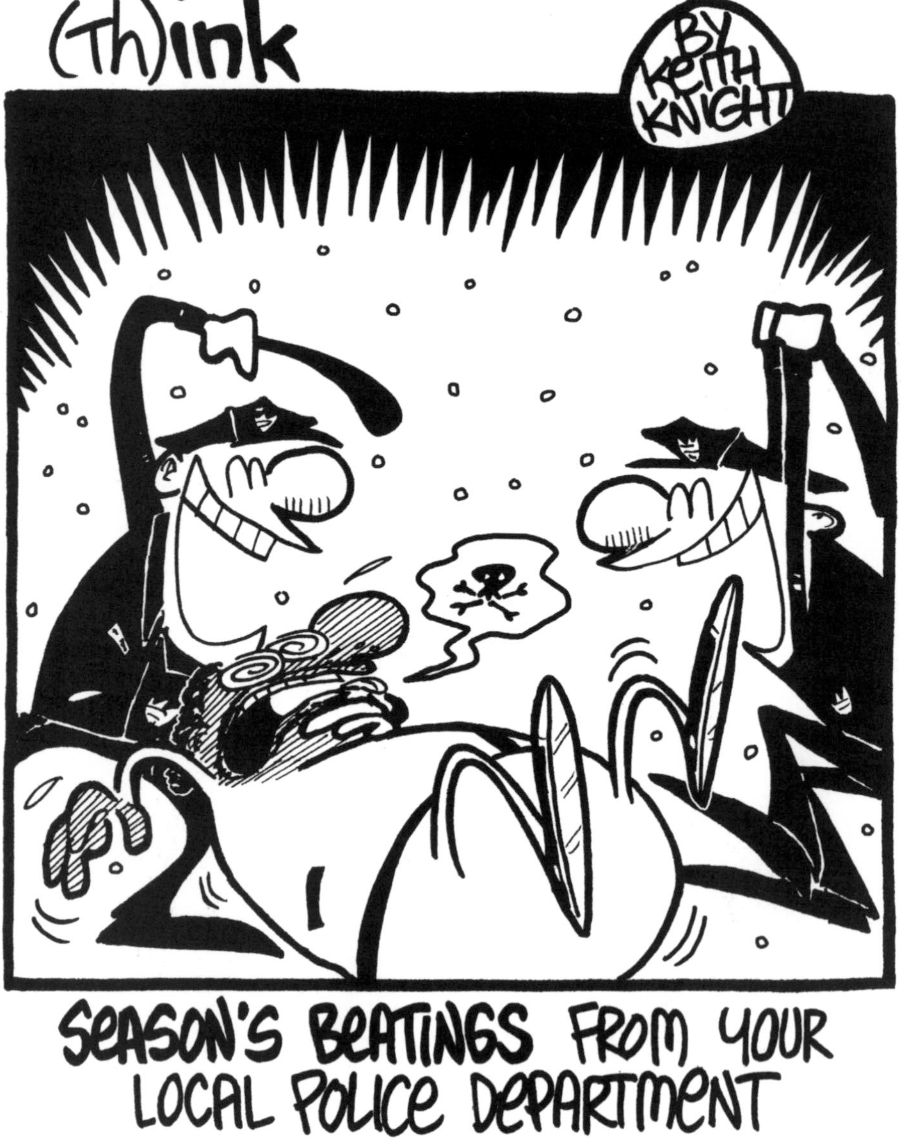
(Th)ink
By Keith Knight
SEASON'S BEATINGS FROM YOUR LOCAL POLICE DEPARTMENT

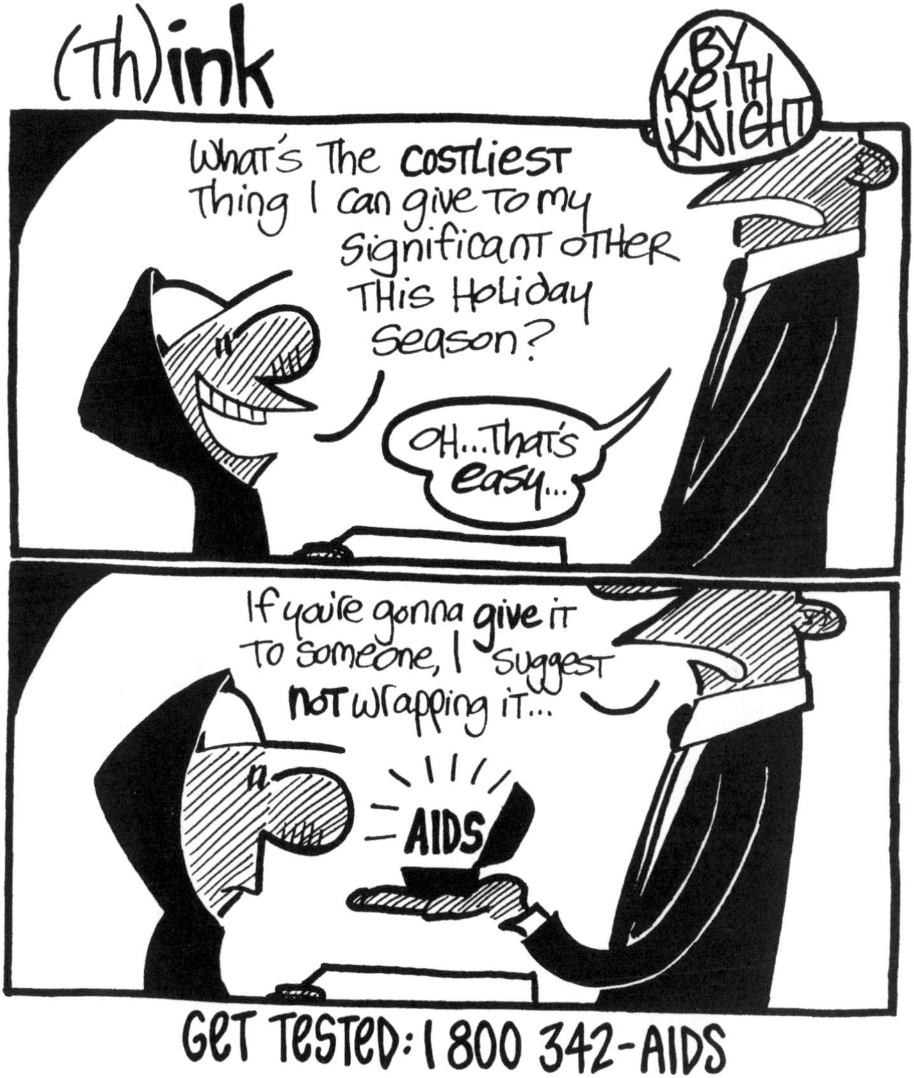
(Th)ink
By Keith Knight
What's The costliest Thing I can give to my significant other This Holiday season?
Oh...That's easy...
If you're gonna give it to someone, I suggest not wrapping it...
AIDS
GET TESTED: 1 800 342-AIDS

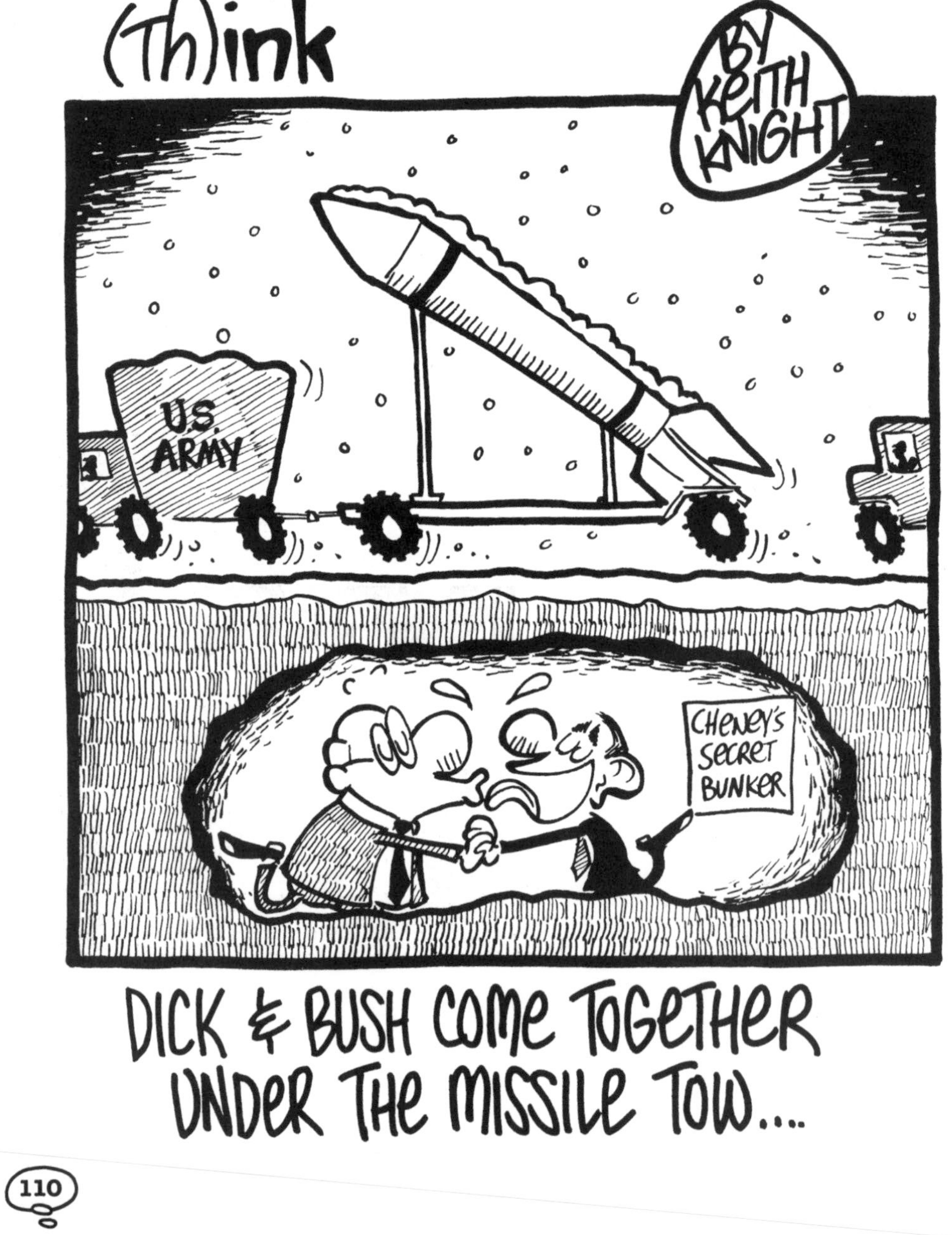
(Th)ink
BY KEITH KNIGHT
U.S. ARMY
CHENEY'S SECRET BUNKER

DICK & BUSH COME TOGETHER UNDER THE MISSILE TOW....

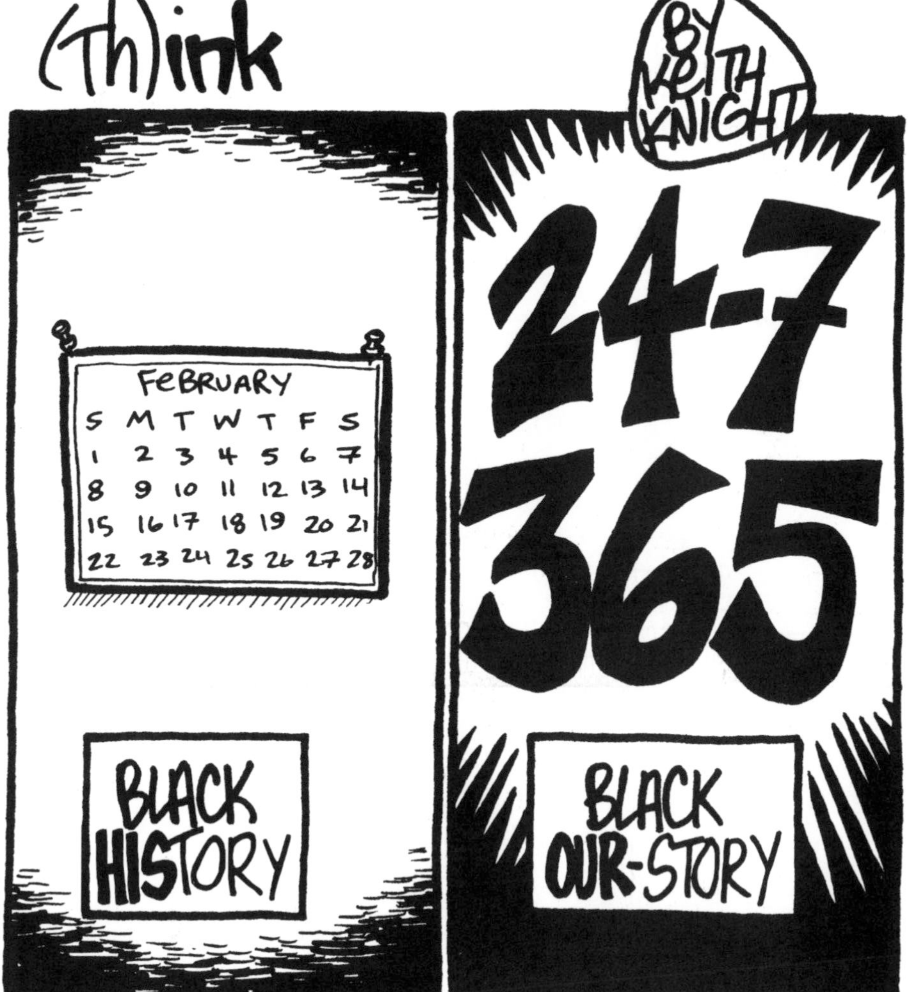
(Th)ink
BY KEITH KNIGHT
FEBRUARY
S M T W T F S
1 2 3 4 5 6 7
8 9 10 11 12 13 14
15 16 17 18 19 20 21
22 23 24 25 26 27 28
BLACK HISTORY
24-7 365
BLACK OUR-STORY

(th)ink
BY KEITH KNIGHT
THE NEW FETAL PROTECTION LAW IN ACTION
I found this sick, little REPROBATE BOILING THE UNBORN, painting them funny COLORS & then TRYING to HIDE THE evidence!!

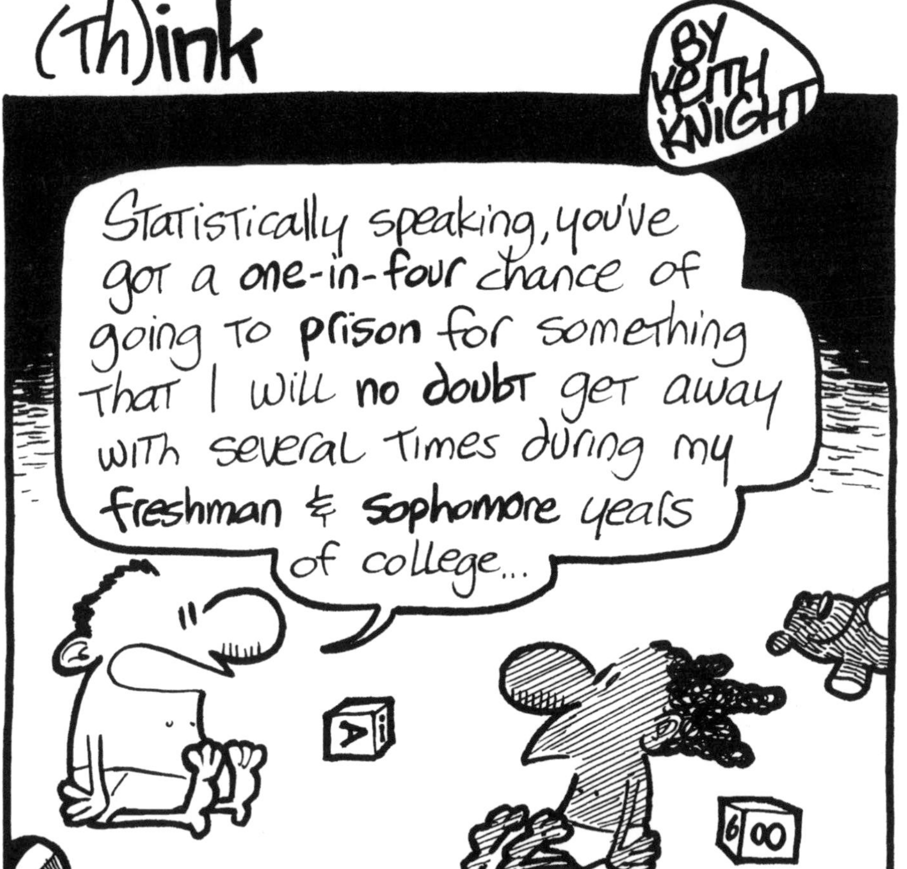
(Th)ink
BY KEITH KNIGHT
Statistically speaking, you've got a one-in-four chance of going to prison for something that I will no doubt get away with several times during my freshman & sophomore years of college...

A RECENT STUDY FOUND THAT **BLACK CHILDREN** ARE **LESS LIKELY** TO GET ENOUGH **SLEEP** THAN THEIR WHITE COUNTERPARTS...

(th)ink

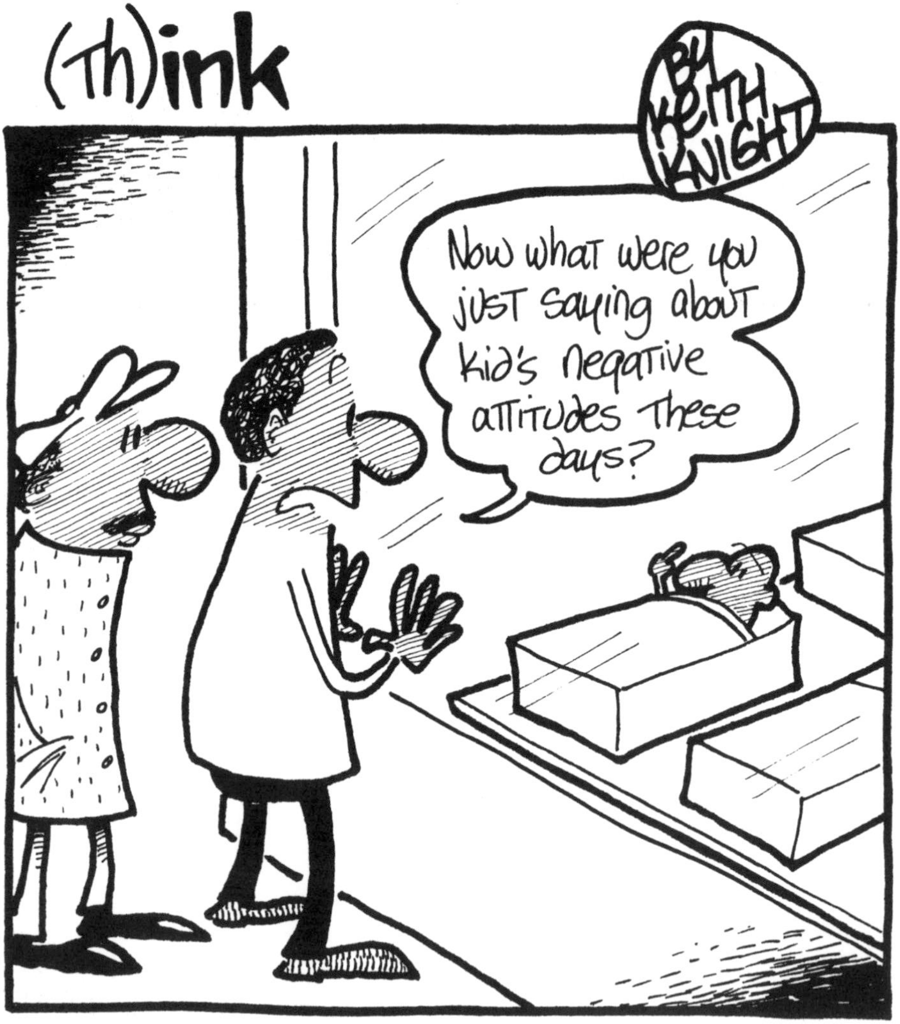
BY KEITH KNIGHT
Now what were you just saying about kid's negative attitudes these days?

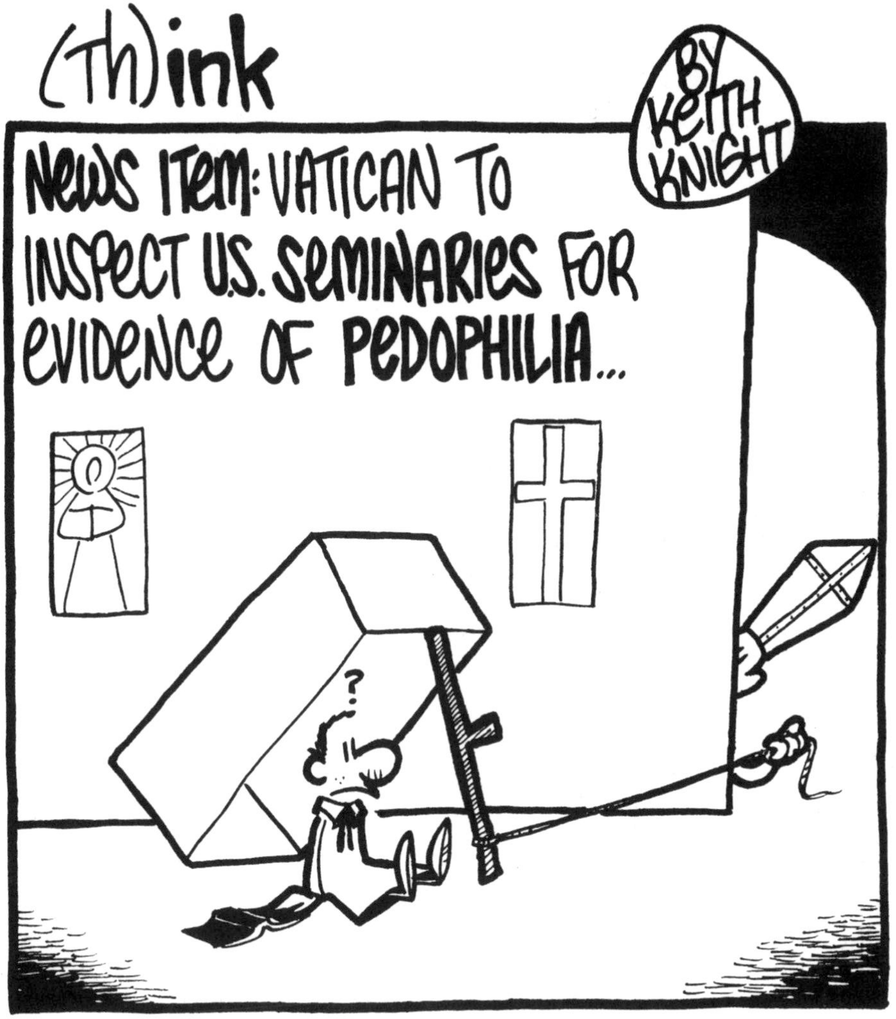
(Th)ink
BY KEITH KNIGHT
NEWS ITEM: VATICAN TO INSPECT U.S. SEMINARIES FOR EVIDENCE OF PEDOPHILIA...
?

(Th)ink
BY KEITH KNIGHT
ACCORDING TO RANDOMKID, A NON-PROFIT THAT TRACKS DONATIONS FROM KIDS, U.S. SCHOOL CHILDREN DONATED MORE MONEY TO KATRINA VICTIMS THAN MOST U.S. CORPORATIONS... INCLUDING CHEVRON, AT&T, VERIZON, G.E. AND COCA COLA...
LEMONADE $1 raising $$$ for Katrina
U.S. CORP
Don't you kids have anything better to do? Like drugs or something?!!

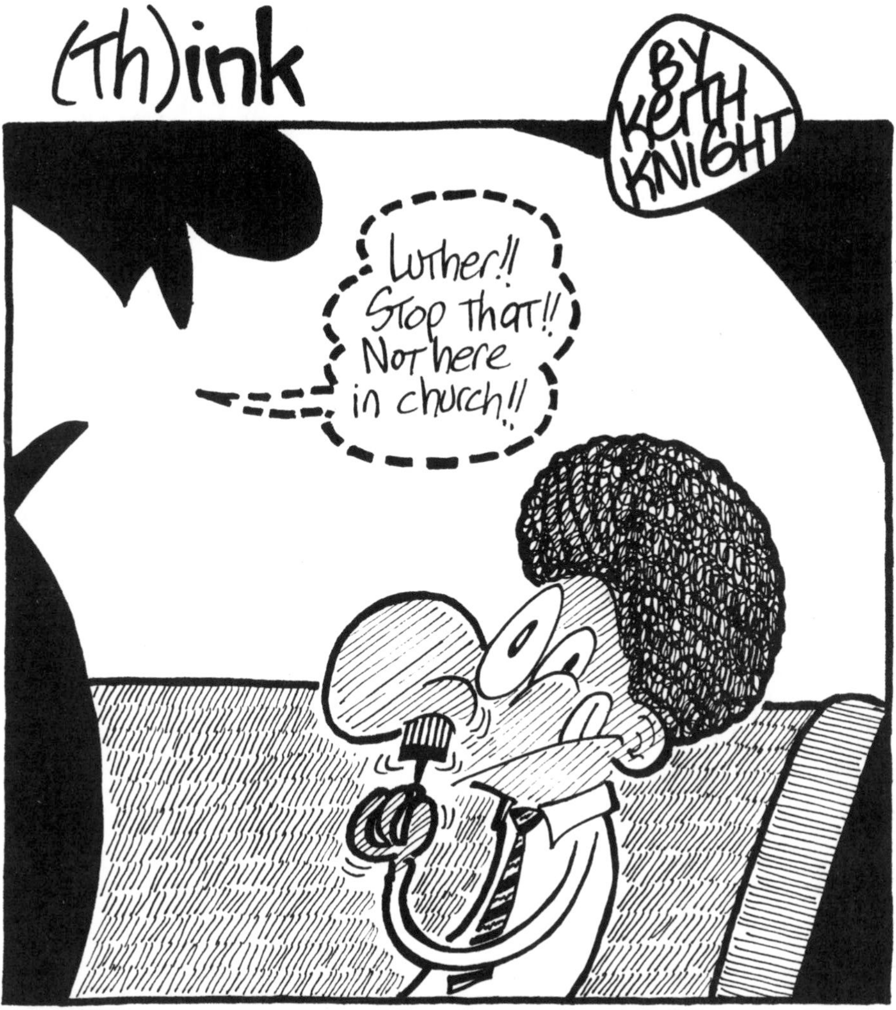
(Th)ink
BY KEITH KNIGHT
Luther!! Stop that!! Not here in church!!

PICKIN' YER NOSE, BACK IN THE DAY

(Th)ink
BY KEITH KNIGHT
NEWS ITEM: 4 OUT OF 5 NASCAR FANS AGAINST RACE-MIXING...
You get These Formula One & I.R.L. posters off The wall or I'LL Throw you out This Trailer, Y'hear me?
BUT, DADDY!!
MICHAEL
F1
RICK

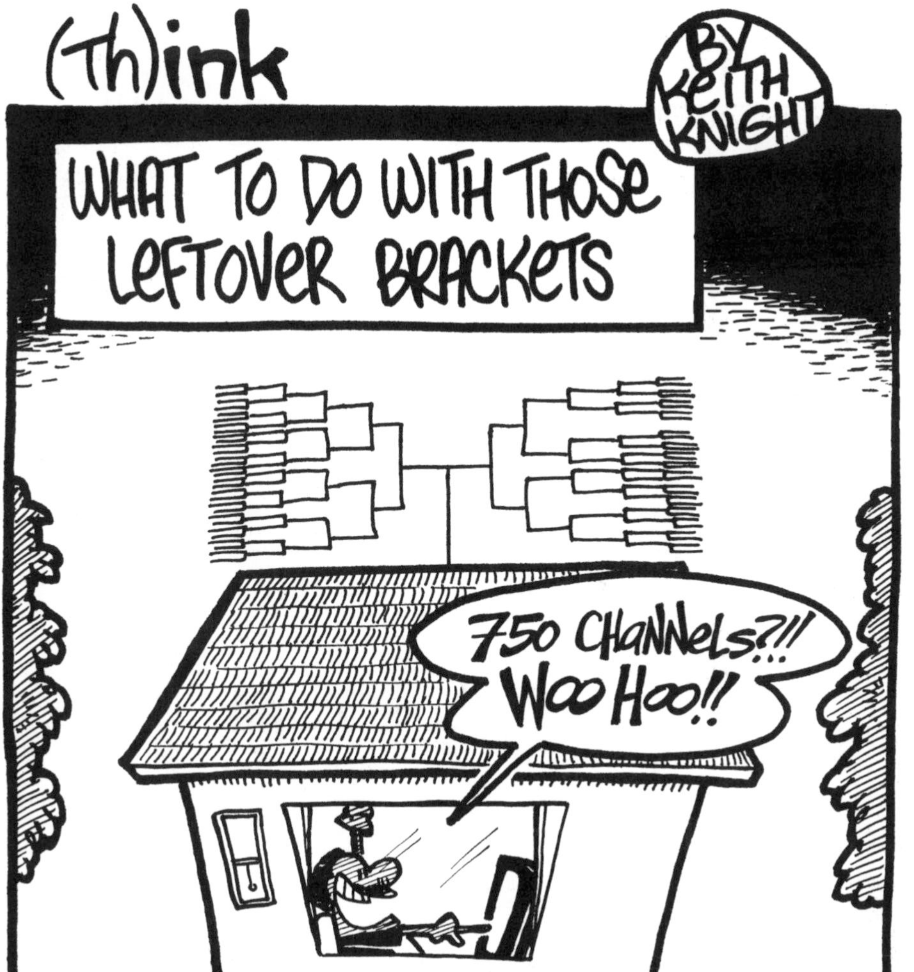
(Th)ink
BY KEITH KNIGHT
WHAT TO DO WITH THOSE LEFTOVER BRACKETS
750 CHANNELS?!! WOO HOO!!

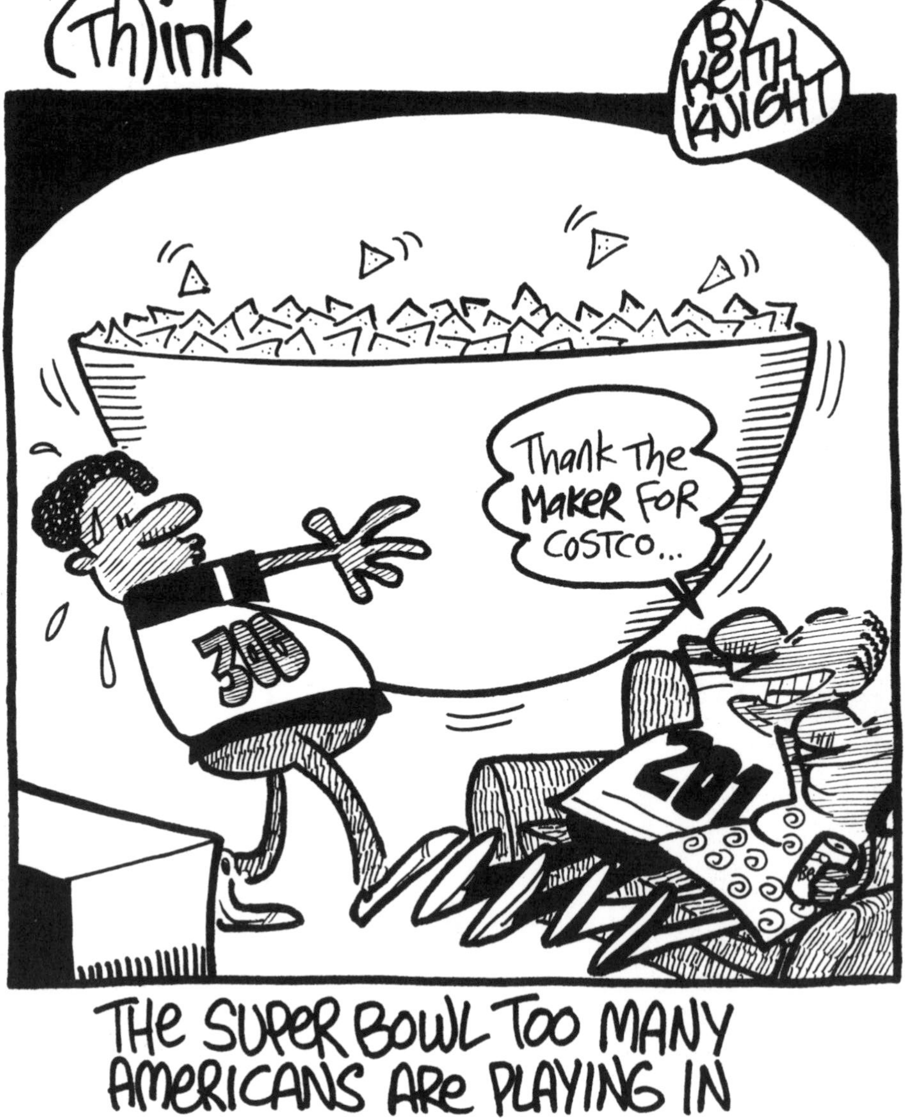
(Th)ink
BY KEITH KNIGHT
Thank The MAKER FOR COSTCO...
300
201
THE SUPER BOWL TOO MANY AMERICANS ARE PLAYING IN

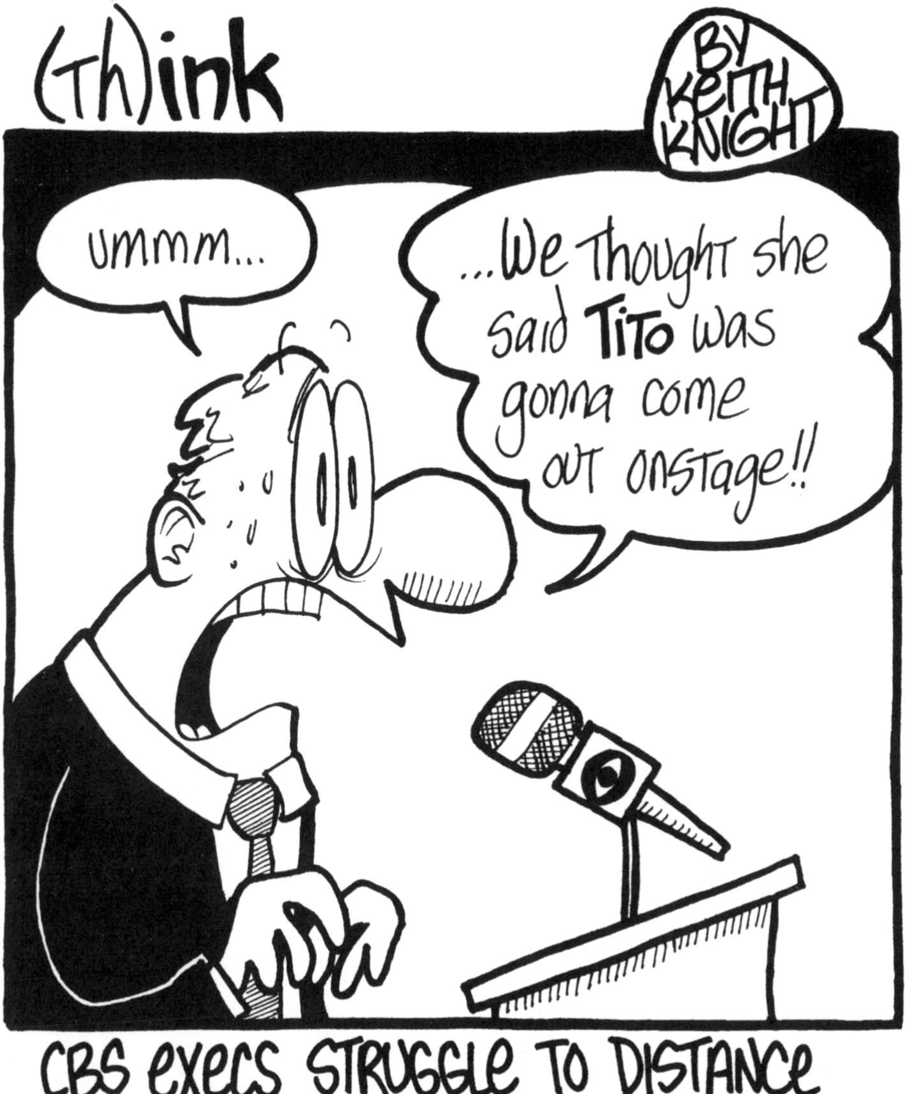
(th)ink
BY KEITH KNIGHT
ummm...
...We thought she said TITO was gonna come out onstage!!

CBS execs struggle to distance themselves from the Janet Jackson debacle..

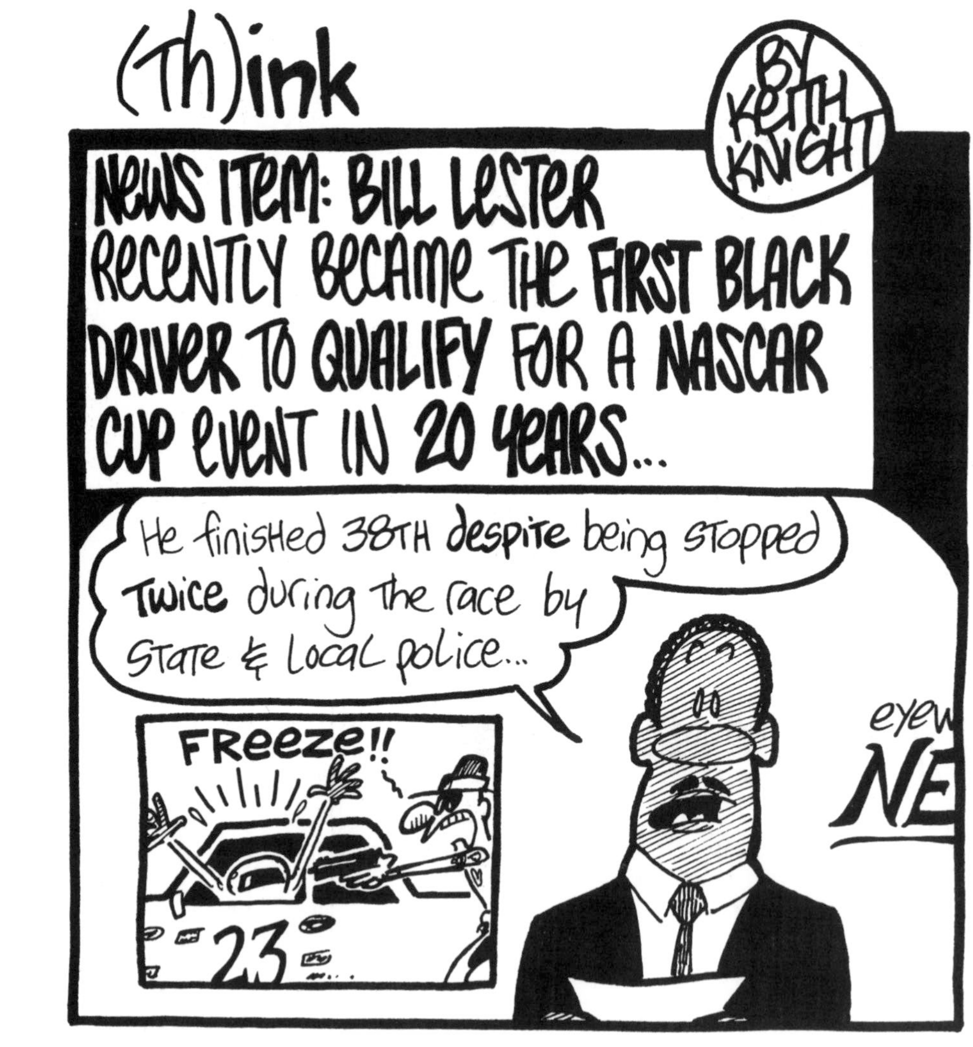

(Th)ink
BY KEITH KNIGHT
NEWS ITEM: BILL LESTER RECENTLY BECAME THE FIRST BLACK DRIVER TO QUALIFY FOR A NASCAR CUP EVENT IN 20 YEARS...
He finished 38TH despite being stopped Twice during the race by State & Local police...
FREEZE!!
23
eyew
NE

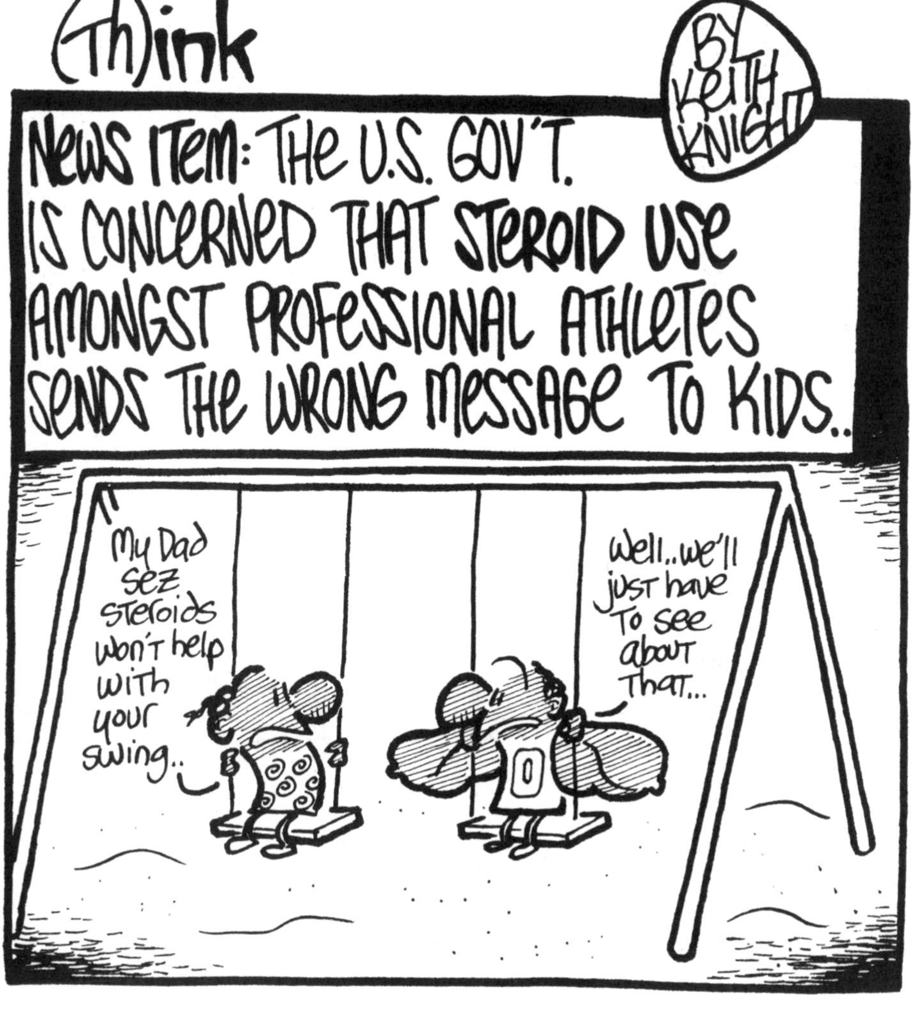
(Th)ink
BY KEITH KNIGHT
NEWS ITEM: THE U.S. GOV'T. IS CONCERNED THAT STEROID USE AMONGST PROFESSIONAL ATHLETES SENDS THE WRONG MESSAGE TO KIDS..
My Dad sez steroids won't help with your swing..
Well..we'll just have to see about that...

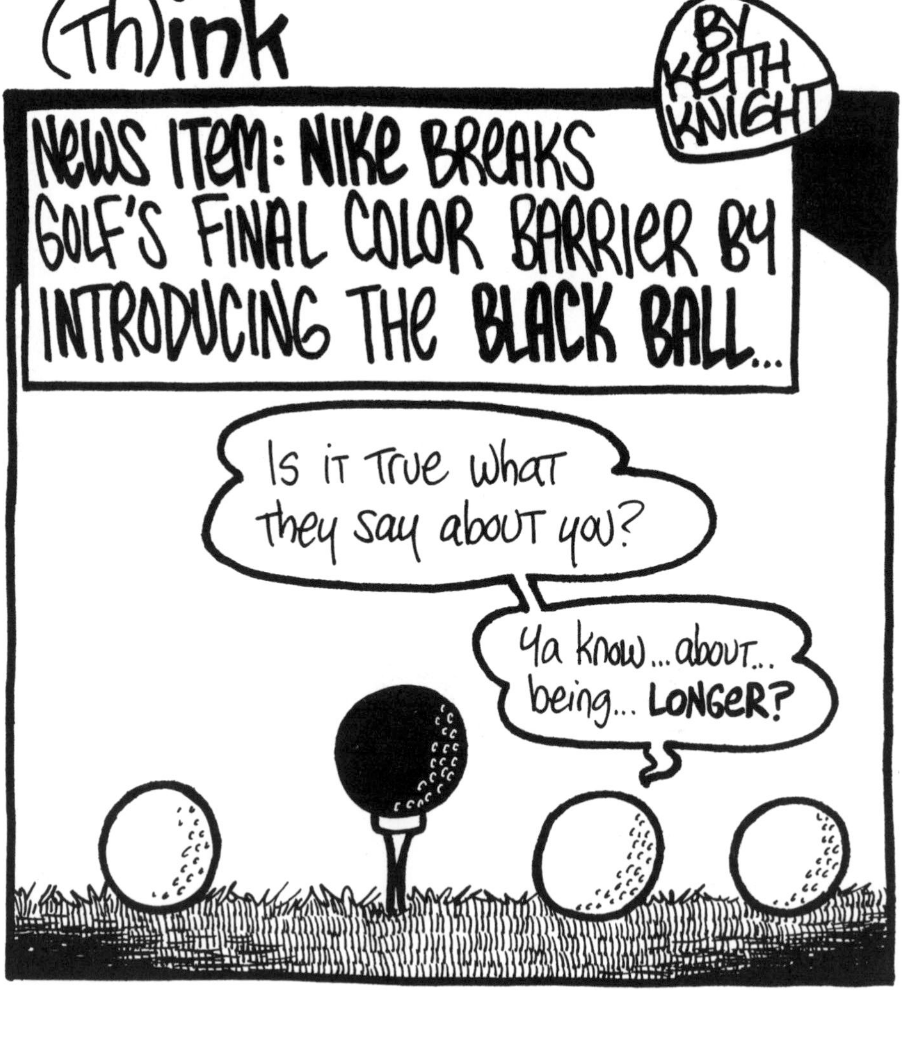
(Th)ink
By Keith Knight
News Item: Nike breaks golf's final color barrier by introducing the BLACK BALL...
Is it true what they say about you?
Ya know... about... being... LONGER?

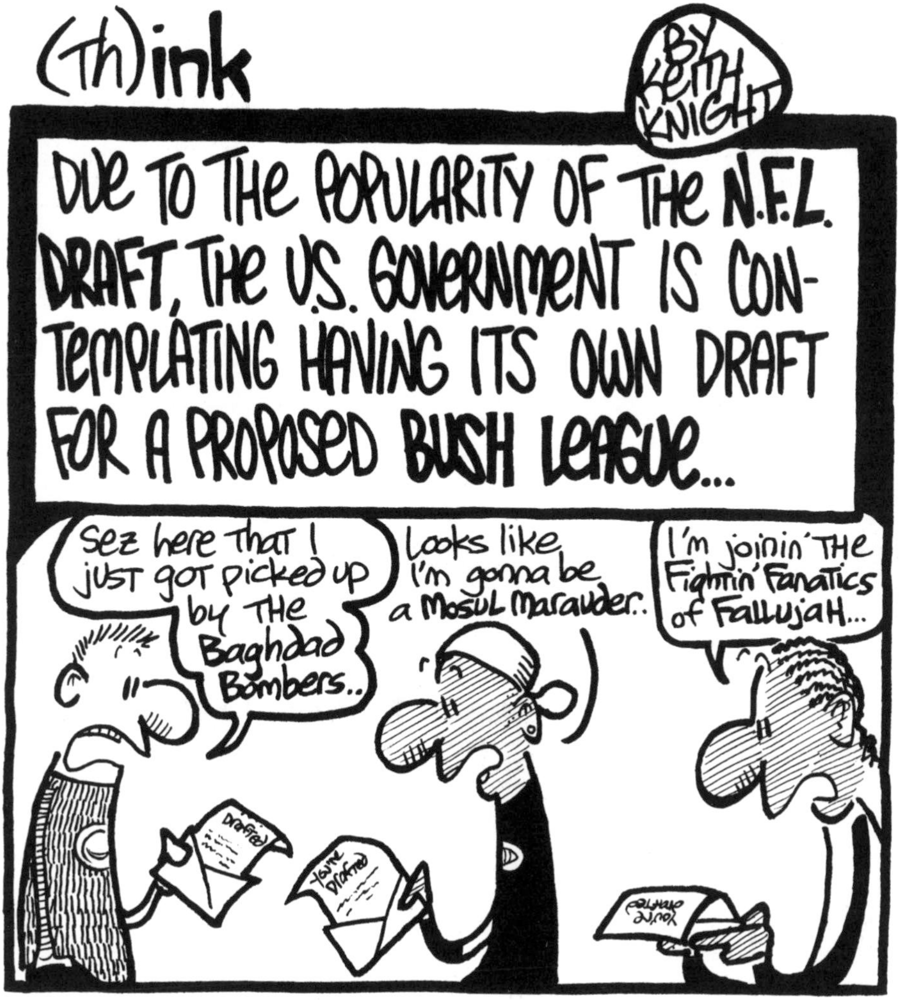
(Th)ink
BY KEITH KNIGHT
DUE TO THE POPULARITY OF THE N.F.L. DRAFT, THE U.S. GOVERNMENT IS CONTEMPLATING HAVING ITS OWN DRAFT FOR A PROPOSED BUSH LEAGUE...
Sez here that I just got picked up by the Baghdad Bombers..
Looks like I'm gonna be a Mosul Marauder..
I'm joinin' the Fightin' Fanatics of Fallujah...
Drafted
You're Drafted
You're drafted

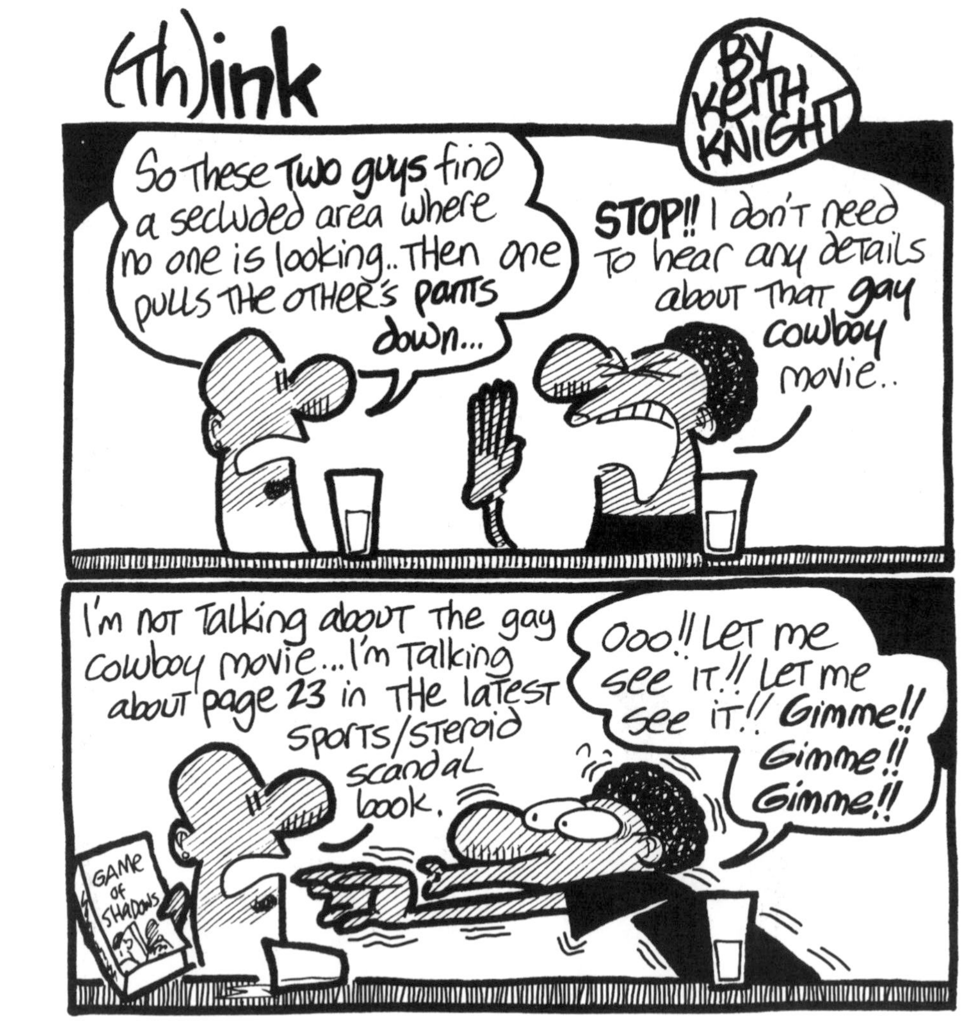
(Th)ink
BY KEITH KNIGHT
So These TWO guys find a secluded area where no one is looking.. THen one pulls THE OTHER'S pants down...
STOP!! I don't need To hear any details about That gay cowboy movie..
I'm not Talking about The gay cowboy movie... I'm Talking about page 23 in THe latest sports/steroid scandal book.
Ooo!! Let me see it!! Let me see it!! Gimme!! Gimme!! Gimme!!
GAME OF SHADOWS

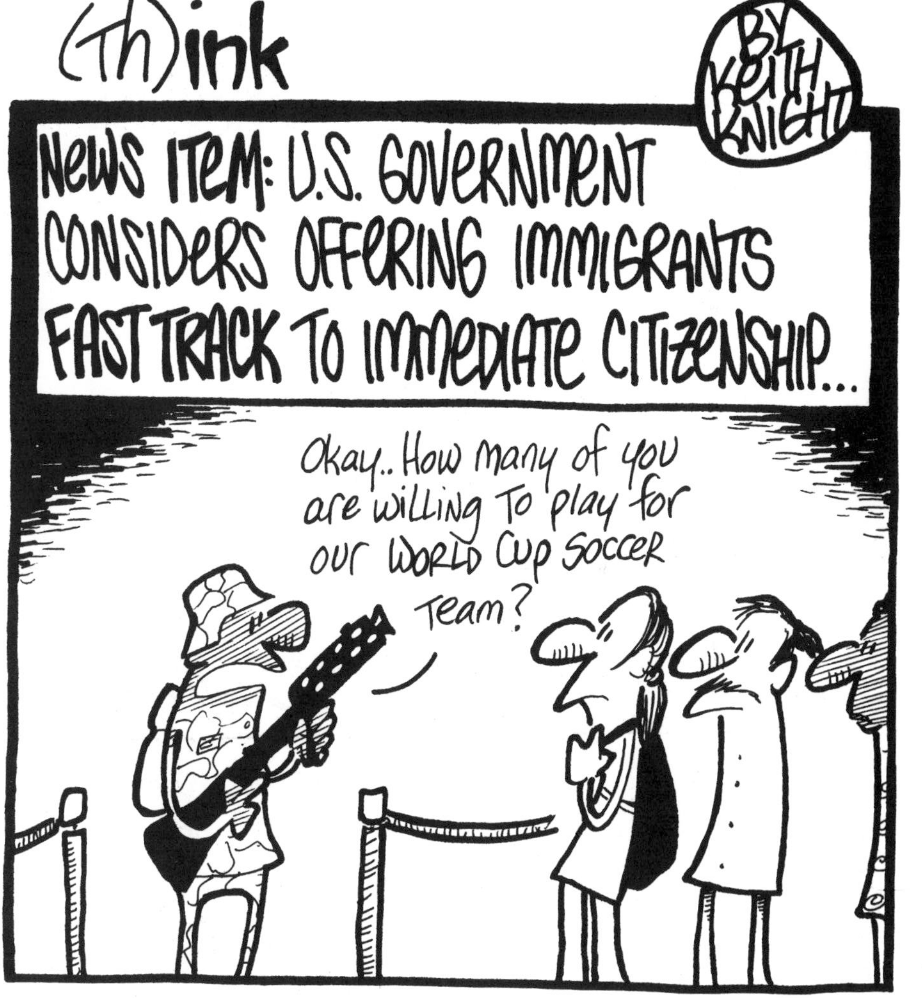
(Th)ink
BY KEITH KNIGHT
NEWS ITEM: U.S. GOVERNMENT CONSIDERS OFFERING IMMIGRANTS FAST TRACK TO IMMEDIATE CITIZENSHIP...
Okay.. How many of you are willing to play for our WORLD CUP SOCCER Team?

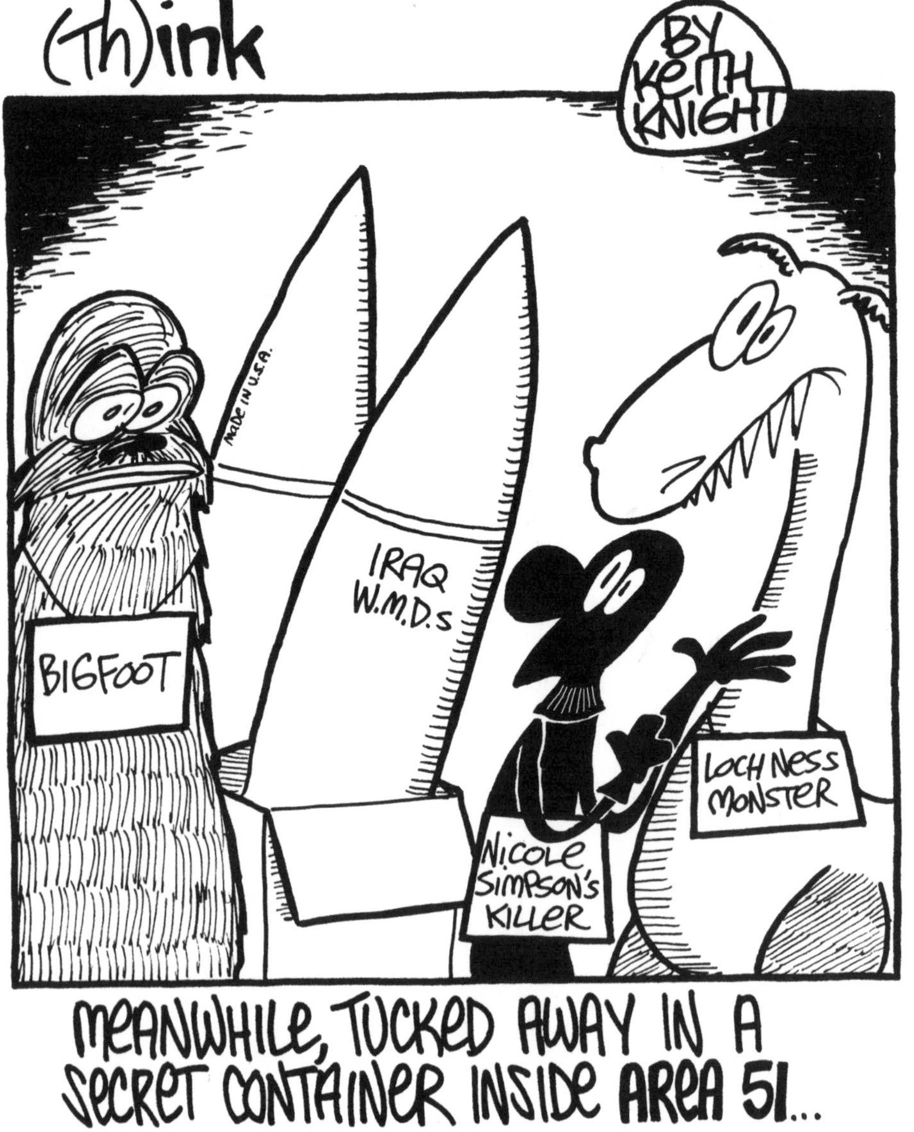
(Th)ink
BY KEITH KNIGHT
MADE IN U.S.A.
IRAQ W.M.D.s
BIGFOOT
LOCH NESS MONSTER
NICOLE SIMPSON'S KILLER
MEANWHILE, TUCKED AWAY IN A SECRET CONTAINER INSIDE AREA 51...